Ain't Had So Much Fun Since Uncle Quentin Died

Also by Tony Deaton

Stop! Look! Listen!
A Practical Guide to Vocal Technique and Performance

Ain't Had So Much Fun Since Uncle Quentin Died

Memories of Growing Up in Rural South Carolina

by Tony Deaton

For Mama and Daddy

…we'll understand it better by and by

Table of Contents

Thanks to...

Sam Venable, for reading, re-reading, making editing suggestions, and most of all, for being a half-decent brother-in-law. When I said to him, "I want to write," he said, "Then write!"

Mary Ann Venable, for amazing design and layout skills, also production expertise, and most of all, for being a way yonder more-than-half-decent sister-in-law.

Sam Hill, for his expert restoration of old photographs.

My wife, Suzy, for her constant love, encouragement, and support, and for listening to my stories for nearly forty years.

Maxie Duke, Cissy Moyle Terry, Barbara Wilson, and Lou Deaton for historical facts and interesting trivia.

Finally, my brother, Wayne Deaton, and my sisters, Joanne Deaton Fields and Nancy Deaton McAlister, for helping me relive and write our memories of the bitter and the sweet.

First off…

T his is a collection of memories and stories from my childhood through adolescence and young adulthood until the time I left home to attend college. It is not intended to be an autobiography with all the events of my life recorded in chronological order, and is certainly not recorded as undeniable truth. These incidents are written as I remember them at the time, with the thoughts and feelings of that time. And now, as a senior adult, I reflect on those memories and stories with the thoughts and feelings I have now.

When I began writing as a hobby about eighteen years ago, my initial goal was to be a short story fiction writer. I fell in love with short stories in an eighth-grade English class. (Maybe due to my short attention span?) After years of infrequent writing, writing workshops, and a great deal of reading—books and books on writing—I've realized what I want most to do is write my life stories. Therefore, the result of this is that I consider myself a mix of memoirist and storyteller, so this book is also a mix of memoir and personal story.

Most of what is written on these pages is true. By that I mean most of the words are the factual descriptions and actual accounts of events. As a memoirist I am compelled to accurately express personal accounts, yet any good story teller will never allow the facts to get in the way of a good story. This brings me back to my initial statement: Most of what is written here is true. Perhaps a better way is to simply say what is not true to the letter of the story is true to the spirit of it.

Some names, but not all, have been changed out of consideration for those still living and out of respect for the defenseless dead. I apologize to anyone who is offended. As with all written truth, the reader must consider the source. In this case I am the source, and these are my stories from my vantage point as I remember them. I am certain that there are people—primarily my siblings—who lived these same stories and will remember things differently, but this is how I remember them.

If you are embarrassed by what you read about yourself, then you are not alone, because I am embarrassed at some of the things I reveal about myself.

We are taught "the truth will set you free." In my writing, I have experienced a sense of freedom from the cloak of my pretentious past. By peeling away the layers of protective armor, I am made to stand and face myself as, in the words of Charlotte Elliott in the old hymn, "Just as I am." This experience has taken me to the valley. And to quote a phrase from another great old gospel hymn, I have found peace: "Peace in the Valley."

Since I was a small boy, music has been a major part of my life, and I frequently use music and songs to express my thoughts and feelings. As you read, you will find several examples of my use of song lyrics for the same purpose, to express my thoughts and feelings.

While reading Rick Bragg's *All Over but the Shoutin'* I saw a lot in common with his stories and mine. The courage to relate a story, regardless of the pain, is a part of what has defined my writing style. But the main inspiration came in the realization that if I don't tell it, in *my* way, and in *my* words, it will be lost. As with Rick Bragg, I write to "get it down" for all who know me.

I write for my siblings who lived so much of it, that they will remember the good and the bad, and from that will come healing and bonding.

I write for my wife Suzy, my stepson Greg, his wife Jennifer, and my grandsons Spencer and Andy, so that my slice of their family history will not be lost. Like many, I'm certain, I wish I could talk to my parents and my grandparents and have them tell me the family stories. But some of those stories which are a part of my family history are lost. Lost forever.

I write for my friends, my students, and anyone who knows me, so they will truly know me and better understand who I am.

I write in the hope that my writing will have a purpose; that I will have made a difference in someone's life so that they might tell their story with honesty, just as Rick Bragg inspired me to tell my story.

I write because I want to be remembered. And by writing, I know that I can live on through my words long after I am dead.

What more could I ask?

Beware the Ides of March

Mama said my birth was hard. I was, in her words, "fastened," so I suppose the doctor had to "unfasten" me from my Mother's womb for me to be born. She said it was very painful, and I'm sure it was. During her pregnancy the doctor detected a second heartbeat and a twin was likely, but another child never materialized.

In southern tradition, my given name was the abbreviated Tony, not Anthony. Mama said if I'd been a twin, we would have been named Tony Morris and Teddy Norris. I liked the sound of that and often wished I'd had a twin brother. But I came into the world as a singleton on March 15, 1949, the last of four children born to Oscar Harris Deaton Jr., and Joyce Martha Marion Dottry Deaton.

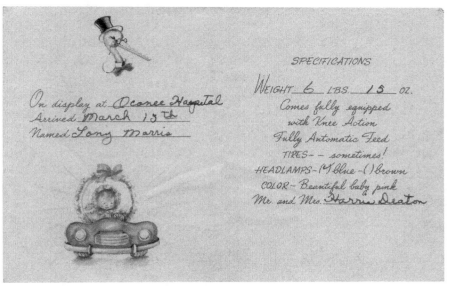

SPECIFICATIONS

WEIGHT 6 LBS. 15 OZ.
Comes fully equipped
with Knee Action
Fully Automatic Feed
TIRES - - sometimes!
HEADLAMPS - (✓) Blue - ( ) Brown
COLOR - Beautiful baby pink
Mr. and Mrs. Harris Deaton

On display at Oconee Hospital
Arrived March 15th
Named Tony Morris

I learned in the seventh grade that a soothsayer named Spurinna warned the ill-fated Julius Caesar to "beware the Ides of March." For what it's worth, I took pride in the fact that I was born on the same date Caesar was brutally assassinated at the hands of a group of conspirators as he attended a meeting of the Roman Senate. As a shy and insecure seventh grader, I grasped at anything for an identity. Every time the Ides of March was mentioned, in any context, I took the opportunity to proudly announce that's when I was born—my birthday.

I didn't know until well into adulthood that I was not exactly a wanted baby.

Only four years and ten months separate Wayne, the oldest of my parents' four children, and me, the youngest. Mama had been popping out babies pretty fast, and I was expected a little too quickly after Nancy, who is only eighteen months older than me.

Daddy's closest friend, James Holcombe, told Daddy that Mama should drink a homemade concoction that would cause her to miscarry. On James' advice and Daddy's stern orders, Mama drank the potion but prayed hard that I would be born—alive and healthy. Many years later when I was an adult, Joanne, my older sister, told me Mama once confided to her that she expressed concern to Daddy about her unborn.

Daddy's response?

"It's just a baby."

Daddy and James' disgusting plot failed, and their miscarriage potion didn't prevent my coming into this world. Mama's prayers were answered, and now I'm writing this memoir.

I never questioned Mama as to why she drank the potentially toxic brew. I assume she was afraid not to do as Daddy ordered, and her faith was so strong she was sure her prayers would be answered.

Perhaps the bigger question is why did Mama feel it was necessary to tell me this sickening story? Some things are better left unsaid, and I could have lived the rest of my life well without knowing that fact about my personal history.

Wanted or unwanted, I beat Daddy and James Holcombe and their evil ploy. Maybe they wouldn't have tried so hard had they known the songs I would sing. My joy and laughter. The summer nights of pure wonder. My friends. My wife. My family. My grandsons.

I was born healthy.

I lived. I won.

Me at 5

Up to the forks o' the road

According to the county surveyor, it was exactly five-tenths of a mile from the end of our driveway to where the road divided—the forks of the road—a half-mile stretch of blacktop and gravel, straight as an arrow. Daddy used to joke he could throw a rock all the way to the forks. We'd egg him on to do it, but he'd just say, "Naw, I don't feel like it right now, but I can do it."

We were country folks who lived on the Old Pickens Highway, about seven miles from downtown Walhalla, South Carolina. But it was no highway, and you didn't dare call our road a street. No, sir! It was a road—a country road. Although we were poor, our family abounded in self-pride—pride to a fault at times—and I was especially proud, and grateful, to be a country boy.

"Up to the forks o' the road" was a common expression for directing the unfamiliar traveler. Depending on his direction, the locals said: "You go up to the forks o' the road and bear to the left." Or, "You go up to the forks o' the road and bear to the right."

Directly across the road from our home was a field of about seventeen acres of farmland. In the autumn, when cotton was king, that field was as white as a Norman Rockwell painting of Christmas morning. White, puffy cotton bolls hung from every plant all the way to the distant tree line. Looking up to the forks beyond the snowy field, on the left was an undeveloped pine forest where squirrels nested in tree branches and rabbits made beds in the underbrush. Then from the end of the forest extending to the forks of the road was open pasture land of green fescue where cows and horses grazed.

Facing the forks on the right side of the road were familiar homes and our red brick church with no steeple. Steeples were for Baptists, Methodists, and Presbyterians. We were Church of God.

Pa and Granny Deaton lived just past six acres of pasture land in a wood frame house with a free-standing well box off the side porch. Just beyond Pa and Granny's, our church sat on a gravel knoll surrounded on three sides by the graves of saints dating back to the

1800s, flanked by the church parsonage which was the home of Brother and Sister Childers, our preacher and his wife.

Aunt Ginny's ramshackle house sat back off the road about two hundred yards. Uncle Odes had died of heart trouble at the young age of fifty-one, but Aunt Ginny still lived there with sons Frank and Edward and daughters Ruby and Edna. Times were tough and jobs were scarce, so Aunt Ginny took in laundry to help put food on the table. She charged three dollars to wash, starch, iron, and fold clothes for our family of six.

My other grandparents, Pa and Granny Dottry, lived at the far end of our rural realm, at the forks of the road. Even though their house was austere in appearance with its cinderblock exterior and tin roof, there was no lack of love within its walls.

Previously, Pa and Granny had lived at "the old Casson Place" about one mile away, where Pa farmed cotton. Granny said the Casson Place was "hainted," but that only added to its charm. Who knows? Anyway, just about every farmhouse in the county was known to have a "haint" or two lurking in the dark shadows.

After the final harvest in the fall of 1956, Pa sold his last bale of cotton and retired. He and Granny moved from the Casson Place to the little block house built especially for them. Although it lacked some modern conveniences, it was their home—the first home they'd ever owned.

To the untrained eye, all one might see in that half mile was our modest home with white asbestos siding, our church, the preacher's house, and the homes of our loving grandparents, intermingled with rolling green pastures, golden cornfields, abundant woodlands, and graceful meadows. But to my brother Wayne and me, it was a world of cops, robbers, cowboys, and Indians. To my sisters Joanne and Nancy, there were the chic boutiques of Paris, the glitzy theatres of London, the posh restaurants and hotels of Rome frequented by famous celebrities seen in movies and magazines. That half mile was our dominion, our kingdom, our terrain where dreams and fairy tales lived. Our Royal Half-Mile possessed the enchantment of thoroughfares that threaded from the tumbleweeds of the Wild West to the castles and cathedrals of Europe.

Wayne, Jo, Nant, and me about 1953

Although less than five years separated my siblings and me, there was a definite pecking order among us.

Wayne, the oldest, assumed the role of protector and sometimes that of surrogate father. He also had a strong sense of self-preservation. After a day of unsupervised mischief, Wayne would pull all of us together and in a hushed voice confirm, "Ain't nobody gonna tell on nobody, are they?" Wayne was also my hero. He could do no wrong. He was blessed with a shock of black, wavy hair, and a well-balanced head of wisdom and good humor. I guess he was good-looking, because all the girls liked him.

Joanne—we called her Jo—was the most intellectual of the four of us. She took school work seriously, made good grades, and was well-liked and respected by both her teachers and her peers. Even though I was impressed by her academic achievements, her dedication to learning didn't rub off on me until much later.

Nancy ("Nant") was also smart and quick-witted. She always looked on the bright side of things. "A whippin' don't last forever," was Nant's defense against the rigid, overbearing discipline dealt by a rigid, overbearing parent. Nant was only eighteen months older than me, and as kids we were virtual twins, or what some call "Irish twins." With pasteboard boxes, blocks, and rocks we built homes and villages, played with cars and trucks, and for hours and hours lived in a fantasyland. Some of the sweetest memories of my childhood are those of Nant and me playing together.

Both of my sisters were cute, but I didn't know it. What boy thinks his sisters are cute?

And then there was me, Tony. They called me the "baby of the family" and although I hated it, I guess it had its privileges. Wayne, Jo, and Nant would get me to ask Mama and Daddy for favors on their behalf, because they thought the odds were greater if the request came from the baby of the family.

To this day I've never seen one baby picture of myself, but I'd like to think I was "just adorable." Adorable or not, I was sure one sick infant. I had seizures that scared Mama and Daddy to death, and I would sometimes hold my breath until I turned purple.

On one occasion I held my breath so long that after slaps and shakes and prayers of "Oh Lord, please make him breathe!" they thought I was pretty near a goner. There was a revival service being held at the church, so Mama and Daddy rushed to the car with me in Mama's arms and sped toward the church to have the preacher pray for me. On the way, Daddy hit a big bump in the road, and the jolt caused me to catch my breath.

I lived to tell about it.

We were not a full-time farm family, but we depended on the land and livestock for a good portion of our modest diet. We had a milk cow, a flock of chickens, a few hogs, and every summer, a huge vegetable garden. Our milk cow was named Junie—she was born in the month of June—the offspring of Julie, who was born in July. Wayne milked Junie every morning before breakfast, and every night before supper, and we drank her milk daily. When I was too young to milk, to keep Junie from swatting her long hairy tail in Wayne's face, I was designated as the ever-present official "cow tail holder."

From Wayne's lightning quick grips, snow-white foam fashioned a creamy froth as Junie's milk rose, inch by inch, to the top of the metal bucket. I was introduced to the ways of the world by Big Brother as Wayne and I had many a brother-to-brother talk to the steady, rhythmic background of udder music.

It's a wonder poor ol' Junie survived Wayne and me. The slightest offense such as a herky-jerky twitch, or worst of all, stepping in the milk bucket, brought our wrath down on her with little mercy. At the slightest provocation, a stout stick was handy for a vicious swat.

It never occurred to Wayne and me that we were abusing the very thing that provided us daily nourishment. But with Daddy as a role model, reason, rationale, patience, and kindness (much less "be kind to animals") were traits not often exhibited, and we learned by example.

However, faithful she was; Junie gave her milk down, and we drank it. "Pasture-ized milk" we called it. And it was: straight from the pasture, through Junie's udders, into the milk bucket, and onto our supper table.

Every once in a while Junie would graze on a patch of bitter weeds, and could you ever more taste them in the milk. Bitter! But we drank it anyway—had to if we wanted milk. We even made ice cream with bitter weed milk, but the vanilla extract couldn't compete with the potent bitter weeds.

We had buttermilk, too. I can still see Mama sitting on the side porch churning milk by hand with the wooden paddle; up-and-down, up-and-down in a tall, pale blue milk urn. Mama's buttermilk had tiny chunks of butter in it, and it was the best buttermilk you could find. Lord, it was good!

Country living was especially good during the summer. Although it was hot and humid, the days were fun—no school and long daylight hours. No one had air conditioning, not even the rich folks, so during summer months the windows were open to allow as much ventilation as possible.

Every night, Mother Nature presented a spectacle of sight and sound as the katydids' rhythmic chick-a-chee, chick-a-chee, chick-a-chee accompanied the chirp, chirp, chirping crickets and the croaking tree frogs, all set against a magical backdrop of endless blinking lightning bugs. On quiet nights you could hear the distant lowing of a cow or a pack of hounds chasing a fox. But the sweetest sound of all was the plaintive song of the whip-poor-will (pronounced "whipperwheel") which sang all night long. Once a whip-poor-will starts, it can call, non-stop, hundreds of times without seeming to catch its breath: Whip-er-wheel! Whip-er-wheel! Whip-er-wheel! Whip-er-wheel!

I suppose that sound could be annoying to some, but it was pure music to my ears. What I wouldn't give to hear a whip-poor-will singing tonight.

Even though I no longer live in the country, I still love summer nights. I never read "Good Night Moon," but often after dark, I go out on my back porch and say good night to the moon, the clouds, the stars, and to those beings on stars—whatever they are—millions of miles away. I say good night to the good earth, the birds, bees, bugs, and to the flowers, the trees and shrubs. I say a special good night and a sincere thank you to the lightning bugs and hummingbirds, who to me are some of the most marvelous creatures on earth.

As I take in the wonders of the world, a deep sense of nostalgia sweeps over me, and I long for those summer nights of my youth. For a moment, I hold tight to that bittersweet memory.

Then, before going inside, I say good night—by name—to each of those I love, those living and those who have passed.

The golden corner

T he Oconee Memorial Hospital in Seneca, South Carolina, was my birthplace, but Walhalla, about eight miles northwest of Seneca, is my hometown.

Walhalla was settled in 1850 by a band of first-generation Germans from Charleston, led by General John A. Wagener. Names such as Kuemmerer, Kaufmann, Brandt, and Bauknight are as common as Smith and Jones in the little town, which takes its name from the pages of Norse mythology. According to legend, Valkyries were beautiful young maidens endowed with goddess-like powers, who came down after battles and gathered all the dead warriors from the "Field of Valor" to carry them to Valhalla, the Garden of the Gods. In Valhalla, the valiant heroes recovered from their mortal wounds and lived happily ever after, drinking mead and feasting on roast beef. The call letters for the local radio station in Walhalla were (and still are) WGOG—Walhalla, Garden of the Gods.

Scots-Irish, or the more commonly used term, Scotch-Irish descendants were also attracted to the rolling foothills of South Carolina. Names beginning with Mc—such as McAlister,

McConnell, McDaniel, and McDavid—mingle with Walhalla residents whose ancestors migrated from other parts of the United Kingdom. Included as well are a small representation of African Americans (I'm ashamed to say that's not what they were called when I lived there), Native American Cherokees, and one Jewish family. Like me, many of the locals are a mix of some, or all, of the above.

Saint John's Lutheran Church, with its gleaming white exterior and blood-red doors, is honorably positioned high and proud in the center of Walhalla. Gracious palmetto trees along the divided lanes of Main Street nod to this venerable, sacred edifice and extend north to the obelisk monument erected in honor of General Wagener.

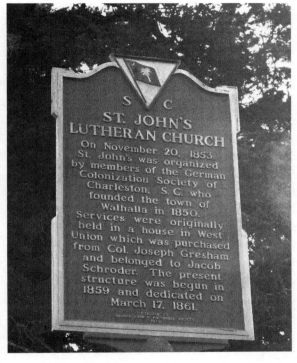

Once, Main Street was lined with elegant antebellum homes and storefronts with grand Victorian facades—an idyllic old southern town oozing with grace and charm. But grace and charm surrendered to growth and change during the decade of the 1960s. With no apparent respect for family history, architectural history, or any other kind of history, homes that had endured with honor for more than a century were reduced to disgraceful piles of rubble in a matter of hours, while onlookers delighted in the dawn of the modern era, the new South. Sadly, "'Bout time we got rid o' some o' them ol' houses," was the prevailing attitude.

New-model Fords were parked in perfect rows on what was once the footprint of the old Strother house. Now it's nothing but an empty lot. Arby's Roast Beef occupies the space where William Darby's fine home once stood. Those and others are gone. Or, as Margaret Mitchell said, "Gone With the Wind."

Maybe local officials of the '60s were worried about attracting too many tourists to our

lovely town nestled at the foot of the Blue Ridge Mountains.

If that was their goal, they succeeded.

Bauknight House

South Carolina has three diverse regions: The low country, the piedmont, and the upstate. Each region has its own distinctive traits and takes pride in its individual topography, styles of barbeque, and speech accents. When it comes to speaking, the people where I'm from seem to have a love affair with the letter "r." If a word has an "r", the "r" is given a great deal of emphasis.

In *All Over but the Shoutin'* Rick Bragg writes about his grandfather, who "stuck the r in even where it don't need to be…" I heard this use of the extra "r" in names of people and places where I grew up. For example, Linda and Brenda were Linder and Brender. (To "er" is Southern.) The three main towns of Oconee County— Walhalla, Seneca, and Westminster—are often pronounced by the locals as Walhaller, Sinnicker, and Westminister (with the added "i" as in minister, a preacher.)

I have my own unscientific conclusions about the attention given to the "r" in the various regions of the South. It makes sense to me that it comes from the influence of the Scotch-Irish. Consider Mary Queen of Scots, who was referred to as "The Queen of all Argyle" (pronounced "Arrrgyle," like a pirate's "arrrgh!") It was those descendants who settled into the mountains and foothills of southern Appalachia.

Georgia claims "The Peach State" as its slogan, but everyone who loves sweet, juicy, southern peaches knows the best peaches in the entire country come from "The Palmetto State," South Carolina.

Oconee County is also known for its apples. Dozens of orchards of Red Delicious, Golden Delicious, Granny Smith, Winesap, and other apple varieties are set in the Long Creek community between Westminster, South Carolina, and Clayton, Georgia.

Oconee County is northwest of Greenville, and is ideally located in the corner of the triangle shaped state. "The Golden Corner," as it's called, borders North Carolina to the north and Georgia to the west, and is as "upstate" as it can be in South Carolina. Man-made and God-made crystal lakes and rivers, lush green meadows, and spectacular cascading waterfalls offer some of the most beautiful scenery found anywhere in America. Each spring the Oconee Bell, a rare flower named for the county, delights the locals with its white and yellow blossoms, red stems, and red-tinged leaves.

Oconee Station

The county is also home to historic Oconee Station. According to SKIWAY or South Carolina Information Highway, in 1792 a blockhouse was built as a military post for settlers' protection against the Cherokees. Ironically, the same blockhouse later served to protect Indians against settler encroachment.

Another Oconee County historic site is the Stumphouse Mountain Tunnel, situated about seven miles northwest of Walhalla on Highway 28. The tunnel was first proposed in 1835 by residents of Charleston as a route for the Blue Ridge Railroad. Construction began in 1852 with the intention to cross the Blue Ridge Mountains through the Carolinas, into Tennessee, and eventually to Cincinnati. Unfortunately, the outbreak of the Civil War in 1861and a lack of funds brought construction to a halt. Following the end of the Civil War, an attempt to resume work was again abandoned due to the depressed postwar economy, and completion of the tunnel was never realized. (And to think, had the Stumphouse Mountain Tunnel been completed, I may have ridden the train when I attended college in Tennessee.)

Near the Stumphouse Mountain Tunnel, Issaqueena Falls holds perhaps the most intriguing tale of the upstate with the legend of the Indian maiden, Issaqueena, who warned a community of white settlers of an attack by her own tribe. As she was being pursued for her betrayal, Issaqueena feigned a suicide leap over the falls, but safely landed on a rocky ledge, and then hid behind the falling water. Believing she was dead, the tribe ended its pursuit, and Issaqueena escaped unharmed. The majesty of the cascading falls is a fitting tribute to the noble legend of this courageous and gallant Indian maiden.

A good portion of Oconee County is still rural countryside with homes set near fields of produce and pastureland. Communities, hamlets, and villages dot the landscape with the three small, incorporated towns—not big enough to be called cities—of Walhalla, Seneca, and Westminster. The first radio station in Oconee County took the call letters WSNW which stand for Walhalla, Seneca, 'N (and) Westminster.

My hometown has the distinction of serving as the county seat. With South Carolina's somewhat lenient marriage laws, the courthouse on Main Street does a right brisk marrying business with residents from neighboring North Carolina and Georgia. I once worked with my uncle, Melvin, as his construction company built a fellowship hall for Saint John's Lutheran Church which was directly across the street from the courthouse. Day after day I witnessed a steady flow of lovely young couples drive up with out-of-state license plates, then stream into the courthouse to declare their nuptials before the presiding probate judge.

Oconee County was a safe and friendly place to grow up. There were no locks on the doors of our country house, and the screen doors only had hook latches which were rarely fastened. I don't remember that anything was ever stolen. We never thought about safety or security when we were away, even on vacations for a week or more. When I was in high school, our home was remodeled and a new locking front door was installed. Suddenly, a loss of innocence. It was as if the forbidden fruit had been consumed and there was no turning back.

We didn't know for sure what to do with the door key—I think we lost it—and the thumb lock on the door knob was as much a nuisance as it was a novelty. We'd more often than not forget to flip it to the unlock position before closing the door as we exited. The only people ever locked out of our house were *us*.

With so much natural beauty, resources, and friendly people, it's no wonder why our friends from the sunshine state and those from the shivering north flocked to the golden corner of South Carolina. And it only took a short drive to distinguish the local residents from the outsiders. The first clue that a car was likely from out of the region was its vinyl top. Oconee residents had nice cars, but really, what is the purpose of a vinyl top? By contrast, a Dodge pickup with a dented fender and a cracked windshield was probably owned by a local good ol' boy.

Among the locals, friendliness was as common as rain. You either knew everybody, or you knew *about* everybody. Regardless of the situation, formal or informal, everyone gave a neighborly, howdy wave to family, friends, casual acquaintances, and total strangers. How big the wave was depended on the closeness of the relationship.

When driving, the standard acknowledgement to the person in the approaching vehicle was to raise two fingers of the hand—index and middle—while continuing to grip the steering wheel with the ring finger, little finger, and thumb. A three-fingers wave was never used because it felt awkward to raise the ring finger without the pinky. Raising four fingers with only a thumb grip was reserved for a church member, school classmate, a pretty good friend, or someone you were trying to impress. And for a relative or a close friend, you lifted the entire hand from the steering wheel with a little flick and flourish.

Outsiders, take a hint: When driving, it is considered inexcusably rude to not wave with a minimum of two fingers. It may feel a little funny at first, but just do it. The locals will grow to love and accept you.

I remember Oconee County as a typical place with its squabbles and disagreements among friends, neighbors, and family. But for the most part, it was a peaceful place with a sense of community among residents. Neighbors helped neighbors. Strangers helped strangers. Many was the time when a poor feller's car wouldn't start, and two or three guys would appear seemingly from out of nowhere and give the car a shove while the car's owner sat behind the wheel, ready to pop the clutch and fire the engine.

When our new church parsonage was under construction, in a show of community spirit, masons from the area who had never attended our church laid brick all day on a Saturday after working a full week. Masons and carpenters from our church would return the favor as needs arose.

The words to the song "Beautiful Oconee," by local columnist and songwriter Frances Riley Richardson (1895-1992), capture the beauty and spirit of the place and people of my beloved home county:

Beautiful land of old Oconee, home of oak and mighty pine;
On your crown of azure mountains, stars and sun forever shine.
Swiftly along your verdant valleys, crystal waters ever flow;
On your fields and fertile plain-lands, fruits and flowers and grasses grow.
Brave are your sons and fair your daughters,
Famed in storied song and deed;
True their love and firm their friendship, quick to care for every need.
Beautiful Oconee, O sweet land of mine;
All my heart's devotion is forever thine.

Daddy

D addy. Hmmm? Where do I start? He was one more piece of work. We tried awful hard to love him, but he sure didn't make it easy. If there was ever a man with two sides, it was Daddy.

He could be funny, loving, and fun-loving. Daddy loved to tell about an incident that happened during basic training for the Army. While taking target practice, his drill sergeant instructed him to "fire at will." Daddy said, "There was this feller named William, so I shot him in the butt. That ol' boy jumped ten feet in the air." I'm still not sure if that story is true or not.

When he was in one of his good moods, he'd humor us by playing blind man's bluff. It was hilarious when Daddy would stumble around the den trying to keep his bearings, then he'd stop and peep from behind the blindfold. We'd die laughing. Checkers games were fun, too. Daddy liked to lean back during a game and proclaim with benign authority, "You gotta king me." And one of my most cherished memories is when Daddy and I took soap and rags outside and washed the car in the pouring rain.

The main pipeline to our septic tank broke and Daddy refused to call a plumber. He tried to repair it with Wayne and me helping. Daddy rarely said anything stronger than "heck" but that septic trouble pushed him over the edge. He must have said at least ten times, "This is the shittiest mess I've ever seen." Wayne and I didn't dare laugh. Well, not then, but we sure got a thousand laughs afterward. I still laugh when I think about it.

He was also clever, charitable, and sympathetic to a good cause. Aunt Ginny only charged three dollars to do our family's laundry, but most of the time Daddy gave her a five- dollar bill and told her to keep the change. Once on a Sunday school fishing trip, one of my classmates cut his foot and had to be taken to the doctor for emergency treatment. Daddy was not even with us when it happened, but because the boy was in my class, Daddy gave some money to the boy's father to help pay the medical expenses. In all those times he could be the kind of daddy any kid would love and respect.

Then there was this other side—a dark side. We never knew when that side would show itself, and it didn't take much to set Daddy off, so much of the time we walked on eggshells. We did whatever it took to humor the ol' man and keep peace in the family.

Whippin's from Daddy were different than those from Mama. They were often expressions of raw anger, and the evidence of one of his whippin's could be visible for days. Long pants for Wayne and me, and long dresses and knee-high socks for Jo and Nant, helped to hide the embarrassment of striped legs from anyone outside our immediate family.

Some beatings were so violent that Daddy's leather belt actually broke the skin. "Daddy cut the blood outta Wayne" was a statement often repeated in my early childhood. "None of my kids are gonna misbehave," was Daddy's mantra.

Ironically, he also took pride in saying "Nobody ever 'run over' my kids."

He was right. Nobody but him.

Daddy's overbearing and abusive nature was not limited to his children. His favorite target was Mama.

Spousal abuse did not come under the scrutiny it does today, and there were no spousal abuse shelters in the 1950s and 60s. In addition, we were isolated from what little protection might otherwise have been available.

I wanted everything to be OK, so my tendency was to pretend it was, and to suppress the anger that continued to build deep inside me. Logic would seem to say the further you are removed in years from abuse, the less its effect is on you. But you don't outgrow or forget abuse. Its memories will surface sooner or later, often unexpectedly. You try to reason with yourself:

That was a long time ago. You're an adult now. Get on with life. But it won't let you go. So eventually you allow it to slip out in conversations with people you love and trust.

When I first confided some of my dark childhood memories to my wife, Suzy, she didn't believe me. At times she even became a little impatient. Suzy's upbringing was one hundred and eighty degrees removed from mine. She was raised in a middle-class suburban home with two loving and supportive parents. Her entire values system was foreign to what I had experienced. It wasn't that she didn't want to be sympathetic; she just had no basis on which to be empathetic. There was no way she could conceive of the terrible things I tried to express to her.

No one can understand unless you have lived it.

Once, as I relayed to Suzy a story of abuse, she replied rather matter-of-factly, "Your mother could have called the cops." But no, she couldn't. We didn't have a phone in our home, and there was no one close by to hear Mama's pleas for help or her cries of pain. In a church where the man was the head of the house, period, there was little understanding or support. Law enforcement tended to view abuse as a personal family matter and seldom became involved.

That was the world we lived in.

Although Wayne, Jo, Nant, and I saw and heard much of the verbal and physical abuse, I suppose only Mama and the good Lord really knew the extent of her suffering.

With an adult mind, I have begun to understand that Daddy's actions were a reaction to the despair and rage inside him that started in his early childhood. I'm not willing to give him a pass, or excuse him for the cruel ways he treated us, but some of the stories he told me are heartbreaking. His family was very poor and they had little to eat. Once when working in a cornfield for a local farmer, Daddy was so hungry he shelled the raw corn from the corncob and ate it there in the field. Out of innocence, I relayed that story to an elementary school teacher. She asked with complete oblivion, "Why didn't he go home and get something to eat?" I was too ashamed to tell her the truth. There wasn't anything to eat at home.

From other stories Daddy told, I realize that during his childhood he was a scared little boy who was neglected and abused—and was rudely aware of the abuse of others. Daddy told me he would be awakened at night by the screams of his mother as she was being beaten by her husband—Daddy's father—my Pa Deaton. Those terrifying memories lingered into his adulthood. While watching a TV show, I've seen Daddy flinch and recoil at the frightened shriek of a woman, and then say, "I'd put a stop to that."

In Daddy's words, "It was a fuss and a fight from the cradle up." My God.

Daddy at 15

Poverty, abuse, neglect, only a seventh-grade education, and what I now believe was a mental disorder shaped a deranged and sick man.

As frightening as it sounds, had Mama left Daddy and taken us to Pa and Granny's, Daddy would have gone on a rampage. The results likely would have been tragic. Very tragic.

There are many who only saw the lighter side of Daddy, and can't imagine that another side of him existed. But it did.

If you don't believe me, ask my brother and sisters.

As a child who endured verbal, emotional, and physical abuse and witnessed the same to my mother and siblings—all at the hands of Daddy—sympathy and understanding were a mighty far stretch—and still are today.

In my mid-fifties, as a way of processing some of the anger and resentment that had built over the years, I began writing stories of my childhood. At that time, I was not prepared to dig deep into the painful issues of my past, so I guarded my emotions with humor, sarcasm, and cynicism.

I referred to Daddy as a man with "gifts."

Perhaps today, his unstable mental condition could be properly identified and treated, but I doubt it. A person has to realize he needs help, and be willing to accept it, before he can be helped. Wayne recently told me that several years ago, when Mama had taken all she could and finally left Daddy, in an effort to reconcile, Daddy agreed to go to family counseling. Afterward, he told Wayne he didn't trust that counselor. "I could see the devil in him."

A rare gift indeed.

Let the church roll on

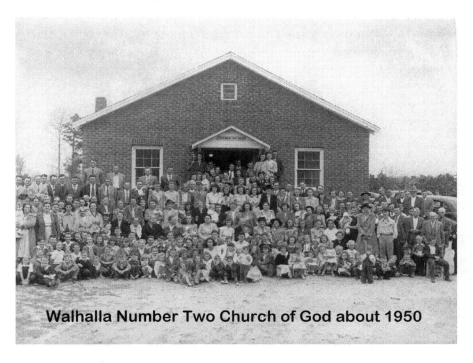

Walhalla Number Two Church of God about 1950

T hroughout the south, and definitely in the golden corner of South Carolina, local churches as well as The Church (with a capital C) in the corporate sense provided the bonds that held a community and its people together. Everybody went to church on Sunday morning. Well, almost everybody. And those who didn't attend church felt guilty because they knew they should. The Baptists not only had Sunday school and a morning worship service, but also a Sunday evening service. Most other churches had some sort of Sunday evening event, as well as a mid-week meeting. The Church of God, where my family and I were members, sort of went overboard when it came to church. We had Sunday school, morning worship, Sunday night preaching, Wednesday night prayer meeting, and a Saturday night Y. P. E. (Young People's Endeavor) service. There were times when I would have just as soon not entered the church doors, but to be honest, out in the country there wasn't much else to do, and church attendance provided a social outlet.

Like most towns of my youth, Walhalla had a First and a Second Baptist, a First and a Second Presbyterian, and a First and a Second Methodist. And even though there were two rather prominent Churches of God in Walhalla, there was no First Church of God and Second Church of God. There was a Number One and a Number Two.

My home church held the rightful claim as the oldest church of its denomination in Walhalla, and in fact, the oldest Church of God in the entire state of South Carolina, but it was named the Walhalla Number Two Church of God. Conversely, its sister church, which was located in town on John Street, was referred to as Number One.

There are conflicting stories as to how these numbered names came about.

One explanation is that a local bank once mistakenly deposited the money in the wrong church's account. As a way of keeping its records accurate, the bank arbitrarily named the church in town Number One, and the church in the country Number Two.

Another account claims that because the rural church was on rural route two, the church was named "Number Two."

But the honest-to-God real reason for the name confusion is this:

In the Oconee Creek Community of rural Walhalla, the first Church of God in South Carolina was organized on July 15, 1914. Although worship was still being held in private homes, the group of eighteen members constituted the first church in the state—"church" as in its proper definition, a body of believers. Subsequently, another church was organized in the town of Walhalla—the one on John Street, and in due time a worship building was erected. Although it was the second church to be organized, because the church in town had claim to the first church *building*, it assumed the name, Walhalla Number One Church of God.

The reason I know this to be the honest-to-God real reason is because this is the story told to me by my Granny Dottry. And who is going to argue with their Granny?

Daddy was obsessively preoccupied with the historic Walhalla Number Two Church of God, where he took delight in showcasing his "gifts." One "gift" in particular was his innate ability to be suspicious of almost every member, and there was one member Daddy never trusted.

Brother Jim.

Brother Jim had sided with Preacher Dillingham in 1951, when it was decided that Daddy's "gifts" were not recognized as "gifts of the spirit." Daddy was told in no uncertain terms that he should share his "gifts" elsewhere.

To put it politely, he was "disfellowshipped" from the church.

To put it not so politely, he was turned out and kicked out. As the old gospel hymn suggests, you got a brother who refuses to do right, you turn him out, you kick him out, and the church rolls on.

According to the church, Daddy didn't do right so they turned him out and kicked him out and the church rolled on. His church had discredited him as a Christian, so Daddy discredited himself. He lost his way. He backslid.

For over five years Daddy enthusiastically engaged in the life of a backslider—drinking, smoking, and womanizing. Consumed by the sins of the flesh, Daddy displayed his sin with no shame. But, Lord be praised, he eventually found his way back.

In October, 1956, a sixteen-year-old evangelist, Lamar Vest, was preaching a revival at Cherry Hill Church of God in the beautiful Cheohee Valley north of Walhalla. How Mama ever convinced Daddy to attend this revival, I'll never know. I do know many prayers had been offered up, by Mama and others, for Daddy's lost and undone soul. He was prayed under such a heavy conviction that he could resist the burden of sin no longer. Although reluctant, Daddy finally relented to attend the revival, and something got a hold of him. There is an old song, "Something Got a Hold of Me," that pretty accurately depicts that night of Daddy's conversion.

After all the preachin', prayin', singin', and shoutin', something got a'hold of him. I reckon it was God.

Wayne, Jo, Nant, and I were staying at Granny Deaton's. Jo, the "most saved" of the four of us, must have also been praying for a miracle, and she was waiting with great anticipation to see if her prayers had been answered. At about 9:30, Jo saw the headlights of a car coming up Granny's driveway. She knew it was Mama and Daddy, so she ran out to meet them. In only a moment, Jo rushed back through Granny's side door, and with tears of joy and relief, cried out, "Daddy got saved, sanctified, and filled with the Holy Ghost!"

In most religions, the next logical step for someone who had just "un-backslid" would be to join—or in Daddy's case, since he'd been disfellowshipped—rejoin the church. I'd heard that the Baptists took in brand new converts the very night they confessed and shook the preacher's hand. And Daddy not only got saved; he also got sanctified and filled with the Holy Ghost—the full dose of salvation in one fell swoop.

I suppose if Daddy had been willing to become a Baptist, it would have been a quick and easy process. Never mind that. When it came to religion, Daddy was a "Church of God is right, hallelujah to the Lamb" kind of man. At least you had to admire his convictions, however biased they may have been.

According to protocol, anyone in the Church of God who has been disfellowshipped and later wishes to rejoin the church, is required to make restitution in the form of a public apology to the local congregation from which he or she has been disfellowshipped. Somehow Daddy swallowed his pride, made his public apology, and received the right hand of fellowship, welcoming him once again into the Church of God.

I guess it's worth mentioning that Daddy later told Mama he apologized "just to satisfy 'em," and he didn't mean a word of it. "I'm as good as any of 'em. I don't need to 'pologize to nobody." Daddy said. I'm no psychologist or theologian—heck, to tell the truth, I'm just barely saved—but I think Daddy's lack of sincerity in his "apology" and his refusal to take responsibility for his actions, could have contributed to his troubled mind.

Nevertheless, Daddy made his public apology, regardless of its sincerity, and his name was once again placed on the church roll. He paid his tithes, gave in the weekly offering, and worked his way up to Sunday school teacher and song leader; however Daddy didn't know the true joy of salvation. He could not overcome the hurt and humiliation of the past. He staunchly refused to forgive Brother Jim for "throwin' him outta the church."

But the church rolled on.

Mama

M ama embraced everything about country living and took pleasure in its simplicity. As she gazed across the side yard, Mama marveled at the fluid motion of sheets on the clothesline billowing in the gentle breeze. She took great pride in the fact she could feed her entire family with the homegrown produce from our garden. Every room in our house was lined with Ball Mason canning jars filled with corn, okra, beans, tomatoes, blackberries, peaches, applesauce, and other fruits and vegetables from Mother Earth.

I loved and respected Mama for her gentle kindness and her keen mind. One of her prized possessions was a report card with an A for every subject, every term, for the entire year. Her intellect was recognized as she earned the distinction of salutatorian of her high school graduating class. Mama was also creative. She wrote stories and poetry, and she knew the Bible like a scholar. She was the standard-bearer of hope, fairness, kindness, and all those qualities my three older siblings and I were taught at her knee.

Of course, Mama's knee was not the only place I learned the lessons of life. With a keen hickory switch across my bare legs, Mama's discipline proved effective.

Mama would sometimes pause in the middle of a switching and ask, "Do you know why you're gettin' this whippin'? Do you know what you did wrong?"

Even as my legs were stinging like a swarm of yellow jackets, my young mind knew it was OK. I accepted Mama and her form of discipline, but unlike Daddy, I was never in fear of her. Her hickory switch was no fun, but I always believed Mama loved me.

Every night before going to sleep, Mama would tuck Jo and Nant into bed, and then Wayne and me, and pray line by line, with us repeating afterwards:

And now I lay me down to sleep;
I pray Thee Lord my soul to keep.
If I should die before I wake,
I pray Thee Lord my soul to take.
I ask it all for Jesus' sake.
Amen.

Mama personified true Christian values, and she taught her children those same principles by the way she lived her daily life. Her generous spirit was evident in the jugs of ice water she prepared and had Wayne and me deliver to hot, weary field hands across the road.

And whosoever shall give to drink unto one of these little ones a cup of cold water only in the name of a disciple, verily I say unto you, he shall in no wise lose his reward.

Matthew 10:42

I was aware Mama endured heartache and disappointment. Wayne, Jo, Nant, and I heard Daddy's continuous verbal insults, and we also knew the hateful way he often treated her. In our own childlike way, we wanted to be Mama's protectors. From the constant abuse Mama endured, her mental and physical health was often fragile. Mama could be cold, and her mood was sometimes unpredictable and confusing, but I made allowances because of the stress she was under. I remember her sitting alone in the metal glider on our front porch, crying her eyes out for what seemed like an hour or more.

I recall one Friday night when I was about ten. Mama was left to babysit her four children as well as five of my cousins who were my age and younger, while Daddy, two of his sisters and their husbands all went out to eat. Mama was near a nervous breakdown. Again, she was sitting alone in that metal glider on our front porch, with an unforgiving sadness on her face, crying while we played. My cousin Darlia asked me why Mama was crying.

"I don't know." I said. But I did know. On some level Wayne, Jo, Nant, and I all knew the source of Mama's sadness.

I was about sixteen when Mama revealed a dark secret that I'm not sure she ever told anyone else. Before World War II, she and Daddy had courted, and obviously in Daddy's mind, they were essentially pre-engaged. Before the relationship went further, due to the outbreak of the war, Daddy entered the military and was stationed at Fort Eustis, Virginia, for basic training. While he was away, he proposed to Mama in a letter, but she wrote him back and made it clear that marriage was out of the question. Mama said she didn't know if he never received her letter, or if he just dismissed it, because when Daddy returned home he acted as though they would be married.

Mama didn't explain why she agreed to marry Daddy, but she did. Maybe she thought she loved him after all. Maybe she was lonely. Maybe she knew her choices of marriage possibilities were limited. And not to make light of the situation, but maybe the sight of a handsome soldier in a well-fitting military uniform was all the encouragement she needed. For whatever reason, when Daddy came home on furlough before being shipped overseas to England, they were married on June 5, 1943.

When I was an adult, Mama told me that on her wedding night she knew she had made a mistake. "It was like a rape," she said. But Wayne was born in May of 1944, and in less than five years, Mama had three more little ones. She must have felt completely helpless and trapped in a marriage she bitterly regretted.

While growing up, I loved Mama, and I also felt sorry for her. My sympathy forgave the times when she seemed aloof, curt, and unfeeling. I felt guilty that I needed her attention when I knew she was so taken for granted and was desperate to be recognized and loved.

A few years before Mama died, I tried again to make sense of a marriage she never wanted, so I asked her why she married Daddy. "Well," she said, "if I hadn't, there wouldn't be a Wayne, a Joanne, a Nancy, and a Tony."

No more questions.

For now we see through a glass, darkly; but then face to face: now I know in part; but then shall I know even as also I am known.
                                                             I Corinthians 13:12

Mama and Daddy courting

Mama and Daddy about 1943

Crazy kids

E ven with an abusive and unstable father, I had happy times early in life.

Once I spent a Saturday night with Kenneth Addis, a buddy of mine from church. The next morning, after getting dressed for Sunday school, Kenneth and I passed the time by rolling a little wheel back and forth across the living room floor. It was a simple game but some of the most fun I'd ever had. I remember the joy of it to this day.

Years later when both Ken and I worked at Lee University, I recalled our wheel-rolling game to him, but he didn't remember it. Funny how kids remember (and forget) different things.

Granny Deaton used to take me "woods rambling." She was smart and respected Mother Nature as a friend. With no fear of the wild, we traipsed among the oaks, pines, and poplars to the tune of mockingbirds and the call of bob whites. Granny identified trees, plants, and herbs with instructions for those that could hurt, and those that could heal. Those were special times with Granny. I wish I could remember all those lessons she taught me about nature and its remedies.

Pa and Granny Deaton

Deep in the woods, Wayne and I discovered an old tire tied to a cable suspended from a high tree branch and hanging in the middle of a gorge. We pulled the tire up the steep side of the gorge as far as the cable would reach and secured it to a tree. One of us would hold the tire in place while the other climbed in. Once all was clear, the tire was let go for a good four or five broad swinging passes. It was fun and it was free.

There were trees to climb, caves to explore, and abandoned buildings ideal for army forts and cowboy hideouts. We found dozens of perfectly-shaped arrowheads we were certain had been used by Cherokee braves for hunting and protection. We believed a tribe of Indians once roamed on the very spot where we stood. That spirit of adventure, to ramble and wander through the woods, is an experience I think every boy should have.

I dammed up a branch that ran in the holler behind our house and made a waist-deep swimming hole. It was little more than an oversized mud hole, but I was proud of it. One of my buddies, Randall Addis, was so impressed with it he stretched his arms over his head and dove in. That took some nerve. But sucker like, I followed right behind him.

One morning when Wayne, Jo, Nant, and I were waiting for the bus, Nant got that "morning urge." In all innocence she told Jo, "Mama said I ought to go when I need to. I'm not supposed to hold it." Pa and Granny Dottry didn't have indoor plumbing, so Nant was going to try and make it to Granny Deaton's, and she wanted Jo to go with her. Wayne and I weren't going to stay and wait for the bus by ourselves while they were at Granny's, so all four of us started down the road. When we were about even with the graveyard at the church, we heard the bus in the distance. Sometimes it only takes the slightest whim to change the entire course of a day, and we all had the same idea at the same time. We darted up the bank and lay down out of sight behind the tombstones. The bus stopped at the forks, blew the horn, waited, then drove past the graveyard and turned around in the church parking lot. But we stayed still. There was no turning back now. The bus went on to school without us.

That evening we told Mama and Daddy we missed school today. They asked, "Did the bus not come?"

"We never saw the bus." we said. We didn't say the reason we didn't see it is because we were lying down with our eyes closed.

Crazy.

I also had bouts of depression.

I distinctly remember telling Mama once that if I wouldn't go to hell, I'd kill myself. It's hard for me to believe I said or even had such dark thoughts. I knew I was sad, but if I could die and go to heaven, that would fix everything. I also knew it would be wrong to kill myself, so I never attempted suicide and eventually "grew out of" that depressed stage.

Perhaps part of the reason for my childhood melancholy was that I could do nothing in the way of normal entertainment. We lived far out in the country, isolated from roller rinks, public swimming pools, movie theaters, and other typical amusement opportunities.

But even if places of entertainment had been nearby, we wouldn't have been allowed to attend. That's because we belonged to the Church of God, and one of its teachings was to "avoid worldly amusements." Daddy's interpretation of "worldly amusements" was anything outside the church walls that was fun. We didn't go to movies, ball games, or county fairs. Nothing. For a long time we didn't even have a television. Life could be pretty boring at times.

During the summers, when Mama and Daddy were at work, we had babysitters. Some were OK, some were mean, and some were just plain weird.

Miss Lusk was a rather stout woman who never smiled. She always wore long dresses with buttons all the way up the front. I guess she didn't wear any underwear. Why? Many times we'd be walking outside and Miss Lusk would stop in her tracks and say, "Wait a minute." Then she would stand where she was, and pee. No, I am not making this up. She'd stand, fully clothed except for under-drawers, and pee right there in the yard. Yep. Weird.

Daddy fired one of our babysitters because she was hateful. She may even have hit us. After that I suppose Mama and Daddy couldn't find a sitter, or couldn't afford one, so during the summer months Wayne, Jo, Nant, and I were left alone during the daytime. Lack of adult supervision did not mean lack of imagination; just the opposite. We created our own entertainment.

We didn't have a swing set with a sliding board, so we made one. There was a drain pipe that ran down a steep bank behind our house, and when lubricated with storm water overflow, it was slick as—well, you know. We called it our "shoot-shoot." We slid down that muddy bank for hours. Talk about fun!

Nant wrote a personal essay for an English class about the fun we had with our homemade backyard shoot-shoot. She titled her essay "Mud Slinging." Her teacher liked the story, but instructed Nant that mudslinging was a negative term used in political campaigns.

I don't think that teacher had ever slid down a steep, muddy bank.

The fun and adventure didn't stop with our homemade sliding board. Wayne stood in a kitchen chair and opened up a trap door to the attic and discovered an indoor obstacle course. As Wayne hoisted us into the attic, he was mindful to tell us where (and where not) to step so we wouldn't come crashing down through the Celotex ceiling. We wouldn't have minded the fall so much, but explaining it to Mama and Daddy would have resulted in a death sentence. We walked the beams with the care and skill of a trapeze artist.

And there were more daredevil stunts.

Have you ever wondered what it's like to stand inside a refrigerator—with the door closed? We found out.

The game was to stay inside until you were so cold or so scared you couldn't take it anymore. Then you were to knock three times.

That's how it started, anyway. But when you have one poor fool inside a refrigerator and three other fools outside, how many times do you think the scared, freezing fool inside has to knock before the three scheming fools outside are going to let him out?

Many. More like three thousand.

While I was inside with the cold and the dark and the fright, pounding the door and yelling, "Let me out! Let me out!" Wayne, Jo, and Nant were outside laughing.

I recall one other daredevil trick. At random, we mixed vinegar, cooking oil, mustard, ketchup, salt, spices, peppers—nothing was off-limits—into a homemade cocktail, and then dared each other to drink it. Man, that was some nasty tasting stuff! One teaspoon at a time was all we could take. And it was rare that the one teaspoonful stayed down.

Yep. Crazy.

When Daddy worked at the Excelsior Mill in Clemson he participated in a rotating car pool with three other men. Each man in the car pool drove his car for a week, then the duty rotated to the next man, and the cycle continued so that each man drove his car one week per month. Although Wayne was five years away from getting a driver's permit, on cold mornings when it was Daddy's week to drive, he instructed Wayne to crawl into the front seat of the car, pull up the emergency brake, put the gear shift into neutral, then crank the car and turn on the heater to warm it up before driving to work. This was a big deal for Wayne. Over time, he grew in his confidence and knowledge of how to operate a car.

The following summer, during a week when it was not Daddy's turn to drive in the rotating car pool, he left the car parked at the top of our driveway, with the door unlocked and, unbelievably, with the key in the ignition. The temptation was too much for Wayne. He knew better than to turn the ignition switch, but he climbed in the front

Wayne and me about 1955

seat, took the steering wheel, pushed in the clutch, moved the gear shift into neutral, and pretended to drive.

Once his joy ride was over, Wayne climbed out and closed the car door. Only problem was, he had left the gear shift in neutral and had not reset the brake. The extra motion of his climbing out and closing the door caused the car to begin rolling. It rolled backward all the way down the driveway and landed in the middle of the road. Thank God no car was coming, or there could have been a crash. Then a saint of a man, Jack Holcombe (distant relation to James Holcombe) drove by, stopped, and asked Wayne what happened. Wayne told Jack his version of the truth, asked him to drive the car back up the driveway, and pleaded with him to not say anything to anybody about what he had seen or done.

As far as I know he never did.

I believe with all my heart that somewhere in heaven there is a Jack Holcombe with a star in his crown.

Pore people shore have a time

O ne chilly Saturday morning, my cousin Frank was helping Daddy and me repair a stretch of barbed wire fence. Daddy set the staple around the wire next to a barb, tapped it couple of times with the hammer, and then gave it a sharp blow to drive it into the locust post. The force of the blow was enough to cause the head of the hammer to fly off the handle and into the weeds.

"DAD BLAME IT!" Daddy yelled.

As he pushed the head of the hammer back onto the handle he said to Frank, "Pore people shore have a time, don't they." I expected Frank to say something like, "I reckon we shore do." But I'll never forget Frank's surprising reply. "Don't know. Ain't never been pore."

I think Frank meant it as a joke, because he was every bit as poor as we were, maybe even one notch lower. But I loved his refreshing attitude, whether sincere or not. Daddy's "pore people shore have a time" was his way of acknowledging the everyday hardships and a way of life where it seemed the poor could rarely catch a break. As sure as you were about to get ahead by a few dollars, something always happened to take those few dollars, and more. Then you were once again trying hard to dig out from under a burden of debt. One of Daddy's favorite sayings was, "Wish I'd o' been born rich instead o' so good lookin'."

I remember the look of defeat and disappointment in Daddy's eyes when he realized he had figured wrong on the weekly expenses, and couldn't make a twenty-five-dollar payment to David Turner. David and his wife, Evelyn, owned the Fairfield Superette on Highway 183 just outside the city limits. David had a reputation as one of the most generous people you'd ever know. He personified the term, "Love thy neighbor," and he helped his neighbor anytime one was in need. David had obviously loaned Daddy a sum of money with the agreement that it be repaid in twenty-five-dollar installments.

Daddy apologized, explained, and pleaded with David. "I thought I was gonna have a little extra this week, but I must o' figured wrong. Can I just give you five dollars this time and make it up later?"

"That'll be fine, Harris," David said.

Yes, poor people sure had a time. Living on credit was an accepted way of life, but most paid their bills one way or another. People drove on recap tires, had blowouts, and those who didn't have a spare tire in the boot of the car drove home on the rim with sparks flying. Layaway was the preferred method of purchasing clothes and goods. Those who had telephones talked to friends, neighbors, and family on party lines with up to sixteen subscribers.

Woven into the fabric of a rich culture were the threads of good, honest, poor people who enjoyed simple pleasures. A cup of coffee was served with a broad rimmed saucer, where the brown nectar would be poured, gently blown, and then slurped across the tip of the tongue. A long sigh and a "mighty fine" was the common response. The three meals of the day were breakfast, dinner, and supper. Grits, gravy, and biscuits for breakfast; beans and cornbread at dinner; and cornbread, milk, and onions for supper. A delicacy for some was a tall glass of buttermilk with cornbread crumbled inside, and then eaten with a long spoon. I once heard a man say in all honesty, "I don't know o' nothin' I like better'n cornbread 'n buttermilk."

There are times when I agree.

At our home, the main entree for Sunday dinner was either meat loaf or fried chicken served with Irish potatoes and English peas. If my sister, Jo, had time she'd make a German chocolate cake for dessert, but dessert was usually a serving of canned fruit cocktail. The preacher's wife rarely had to bother with fixing Sunday dinner, because it was expected the preacher's family would be invited to share dinner at the home of a church member.

In the fall of the year, cotton-pickin' days were as much a part of the season as golden leaves and crisp air. The Keowee County High School closed for ten days, to allow students to work as farmhands harvesting the family's crop. Wayne, Jo, Nant, and I were jealous of the Keowee School students. We thought they got a two-week vacation every October. That notion changed one Saturday when we picked cotton for Pa Dottry. We learned first-hand the back-breaking labor of harvesting cotton was by no means a vacation. The drudgery of school work paled in comparison to cotton-pickin' days.

"Hog killin' weather" was a term synonymous with frigid temperatures. Before air-conditioning was standard equipment in automobiles, the joke was that a farmer was walking to town on a summer afternoon when he was given a ride in an air-conditioned Cadillac. After a few minutes of awkward silence, the driver said, "So, where ya headin' ol' timer?" To which the farmer replied, "Well, I was goin' to town to buy some seed but the air's turned so cold, I think I'll go back home and kill a hog."

When the frozen earth spewed forth spikes of ice, and the early morning frost lay so thick and heavy the ol' timers said it looked like a young snow, it was time for hog killing. As a boy, I looked on with wonder as the innocent creature was shot through the head. His neck was then slit with a razor-sharp knife and the blood, rich and red, poured freely, with a vapor of steam as it met the cold November air. The dead animal was strung upside down with its back feet stretched high, and then sliced the entire length of its body. In routine fashion the entrails were scooped away with skilled hands. As the hogs were butchered, the owner kept his fair share of the choice meats, then as payment he divided the rest with the men who had helped. Nothing was taken for granted, and virtually everything was considered edible. In addition to hog jowl, ham butt, shoulder, ribs, and loin, the feet and ears were pickled, and the skin made into pork rinds. Even the entrails were cooked to make chitterlings, or chitlins as they were called.

I've tried all, and I recommend all except the chitlins. They smell like a hog pen and taste like a hog pen. Give them a try if you dare, but don't say I didn't warn you.

Pickup truck owners proudly displayed their rifles and shotguns in the gun rack across the back windshield. Men hunted game of various sorts—some hunted for sport, some as a food supplement. Rabbits and squirrels by day, and coons and possums at night. Rabbit meat is good. Tastes just like chicken. And if you can get past the fact that a squirrel is nothing but a rodent—a bushy tailed rat—although a little tough, squirrel meat is not bad.

I once worked with a man on a construction crew who hunted coon practically every night. He said his kids loved "coon burgers." Hmmm?

In grammar school we sang a minstrel song, "Carve dat Possum:"

> *Possum meat am good to eat,*
> *Carve 'im to de heart.*
> *You'll always find 'im good an' sweet,*
> *Carve 'im to de heart.*
> *Carve dat possum,*
> *Carve dat possum, chillum,*
> *Carve dat possum to de heart.*

I never tried possum so I don't know if the meat is sweet or not, but I'd have to be mighty hungry before I'd take a bite of either coon or possum.

Those memories make me think of Daddy. Sometimes I really miss him just as he was, warts and all. I also miss what we could have had. One of the first stories I wrote was titled, "Breakfast with Daddy." It was about a morning when just he and I went to breakfast at a roadside diner and had a good time the way a father and son are supposed to.

I wish just Daddy and I could sit down together again over a plate of hot biscuits and gravy. We'd talk about hog killin', living on credit, driving on recap tires, just scraping by from day to day doing the best you can. I think I'd say, "Dad blame it! Pore people shore have a time, don't they."

I wouldn't be surprised if he'd pour a tad of coffee in the saucer, blow it, take a slurp, let out a long sigh, and then say, "Don't know. Ain't never been pore."

Goin' out town

The aroma of fresh-popped corn from Harper's Dime Store wafted its way for blocks in every direction up and down Main Street, Walhalla. Outside the store, a teenage boy called out to passing customers, "We got HOT popcorn ladies and gentlemen! HOT popcorn. Get your HOT popcorn right here!"

That's my first memory of "goin' out town."

No, it's not a typo or an omitted word. It was never going out of town, going to town, over to town, across town, out to town, uptown, or downtown. Our family went "out town." With the crowds of people, the hustle and bustle of shoppers, life-sized store front displays and attractions, and a popcorn salesman, "out town" had a carnival-like atmosphere. I loved it.

Goin' out town became a Saturday afternoon tradition with my family. The Monday through Friday schedule was the same with school, after school chores, a little play time, supper, homework, and then bed. But Saturday was different. On Saturday mornings Mama, Jo, and Nant washed and ironed clothes, cleaned house, and did other inside duties while Daddy, Wayne, and I did outside work like mending pasture fences, nailing up loose boards, and patching the tin roof on the barn and out buildings. This was rural South Carolina in the 1950s-1960s after all. Women's work was inside the house, and men's work was outside the house. But washing the car was a job for all four kids.

Daddy's trick for keeping our car clean was, "You kids wash the car real good and we'll all go out town." Of course we fell for it, because goin' out town was the most exciting thing we did all week. With the brass nozzle on the long green hose-pipe we'd spray off the top layer of a week's worth of dust and dirt, then soap up the car, wash every inch of brown and beige paint, scrub the whitewalls, shine the chrome, and then give her a final rinse. When we finished, the ol' two-tone '53 Bel Air looked as if she just rolled off the showroom floor.

Goin' out town was not just an event for my family and me; it was a weekly ritual for most country folks. Unlike today, not everyone had checking accounts, and some people dealt only in cash money. Although banks were insured by the FDIC and considered financially solvent, the memory of the depression still lingered, when the stock market crashed and one bank after another failed. Instead of a bank vault, some people believed their money was safer at home, under the bed mattress or rolled up in a coffee can.

For a small surcharge, several businesses served as bill-paying locations for various goods and services. Most folks paid their light bill at Neville's Hardware Store in the heart of town. The notice from Blue Ridge Electric Co-op came in the mail on a post card, showing the amount owed according to the number of kilowatts used during the previous month. I remember the smell and creak of hardwood floors with every step down the wide aisle between wheelbarrows, rakes, hoes, shovels, wooden cabinets full of bolts, screws, hinges, and latches, back to the silver-colored ornate cash register near the rear of Neville's store. With the exact cash amount in hand, plus a nickel surcharge, another month of electricity was secure. A nickel would buy an ice cream at Turner's Store, but even as a kid who loved ice cream, I thought a nickel was a bargain for such an important service.

Walhalla was a safe town, so while Mama and Daddy were checking the "out town" errands off their list, Wayne, Jo, Nant, and I were free to wander up and down the sidewalk and in and out of stores. None of the stores had public bathrooms. You either had to hold it until you were home, or be creative in finding a way to relieve yourself. To make the point clear to their customers, Gallant Belk's Department Store hung a sign with letters two feet tall and in all caps between the men's and women's bathrooms that read, "EMPLOYEES ONLY." I can't say that everyone, including the Deaton kids, always observed that sign. When the urge became urgent, we'd dart through the forbidden door to the scowl of one of the privileged employees, and do what needed to be done.

Once a mother with a daughter who looked to be about three years old exited Gallant Belk's but stopped at the threshold. There the little girl hiked up her plaid dress and pulled down her white panties, squatted, and peed right in the doorway entrance. I can only assume the mother had asked a store clerk if her little girl could use their bathroom and was given a curt, "No; it's for employees only," to which the mother must have thought, well, I'll show you. When the little girl had fully relieved herself, she pulled up her panties, straightened her dress, and she and her mother walked away from the river of yellow urine without a word.

Wayne, Jo, Nant, and I were waiting in the car outside of C. G. Jaynes Furniture Store while Mama and Daddy went inside to check out a kitchen table. A few parking spaces over, a man sat behind the steering wheel of a big red Buick with all the windows rolled down. Then a woman came out of C. G. Jaynes and sat next to the man in the front seat of the Buick. While still sitting behind the steering wheel with the woman next to him, the man started the engine, and the rear windows rolled up. Nant's jaw dropped as if she'd just seen a Houdini magic trick.

"Did you see that?!? That window just went 'errrrrnt' and rolled up by itself."

None of us had ever seen a car with power windows and from that point on, they were deemed 'errrrrnt windows.' You press a button, and errrrrnt, the window goes up. You press the button again, and errrrrnt, the window goes down.

With no Walmart, K-mart, strip malls, or shopping centers, the business district of Walhalla was alive with activity all day every Saturday. Our two drug stores kept their doors open from eight a. m. until eight p. m., and most businesses were open from nine in the morning until six at night. Seigler's Steak House served the locals breakfast and dinner, but starting at five o'clock in the evening, customers from as far away as Anderson and Greenville stood in line, with no complaint, for thirty to forty-five minutes waiting their turn for a plate of steak and grits, and one of the finest meals anywhere in the upstate.

Although we were forbidden to go anywhere near it, The Strand Theater showed current movies every Saturday night, and on occasion the Strand also hosted live entertainment. For an entire week, a banner stretched all the way across both directions of Main Street announcing *Lester Flatt and Earl Scruggs Live at the Strand Theater*. Back then I didn't know who Flatt and Scruggs were, but I sure wanted to go see them. And later, when I saw the Flatt and

Scruggs Bluegrass String Band on TV, I wished even more that I'd been able to see them.

We had other forms of live entertainment, and unlike the Strand, these were free of charge. A holiness preacher took up squatter's rights in front of the Arthur Brown Building and proclaimed his fiery message of salvation for a good two hours on Saturday afternoons. Call me irreverent if you want, but that preacher had the look and lure of a snake oil salesman. Dressed in a white three-piece suit, white wing-tipped shoes, and with his shiny, jet black hair, he proclaimed deliverance from sin to whosoever will may come.

And there was another performer. I never knew her name, but a woman who looked to be in her sixties, and was believed to be blind from birth, filled the afternoon air with her angelic voice. I can still see her long wavy hair all the way down her back and her print dress that reached to her ankles. Everyone made a clear path for this sister as she wandered up and down Main Street, accompanying herself on a full-size accordion strapped across her chest, singing to the top of her lungs about Jesus and a heavenly home where one day she would see the face of Jesus with her glorified eyes:

Oh, I want to see Him, look upon His face,
There to sing forever of His saving grace;
On the streets of glory let me lift my voice,
Cares all past, home at last, ever to rejoice.

Those with special requests dropped a coin into the tin cup attached to her accordion strap, but most of the time she sang for free, and from her abundant heart.

She was an inspiration.

Business was kind of slow on Sundays. Seigler's Steak House opened at eleven a. m. in preparation for the church crowd, and our two drug stores opened at one o'clock and closed at five. Red Diamond Filling Station, the only place to get gas, stayed open till nine o'clock. (Of course Davenport Funeral Home was always open, but nobody wanted to do business with them.) Downtown there was no lack of traffic, however. From early afternoon till well after dark, Main Street hosted a constant parade of cruisers. After three or four laps up and down Main, boys with no dates parked their cars, sat on the hoods, and waved at the other cruisers as they drove past.

Small town Americana at its finest.

Come Monday morning, things picked up to a steady but easy pace with shops, stores, cafes, and restaurants open during regular business hours, but banks were the exception. Long before computers and calculators, debits and credits were tediously reconciled down to the penny by slow, clumsy adding machines. Although tellers worked long hours accounting for the bank's assets, the "open to the public" hours were short compared to other businesses. "He's keeping 'banker's hours'" was a term fellow employees directed in jest at anyone who left work early.

Compared to today, life was lived at a slower, more leisurely pace back then. A midweek respite was observed on Wednesdays, when all but essential commerce closed at one o'clock and didn't reopen until the next morning.

Only a few years ago I instructed one of my voice students, who was a devout Seventh Day Adventist, that he should practice every day. He replied, "But I need my Sabbath." At first it caught me off guard, and to be honest, I was a little embarrassed. But I couldn't argue with this wise young man.

Yes, we need our Sabbath, but we rarely take one. More peace in our lives would likely benefit most of us; the peace we knew in those easy flowing hours of Sunday—and Wednesday afternoons beginning at one o'clock.

Y'all come 'n go with us

Where I grew up

W arm, lazy summer afternoons were often spent rocking or swinging on the front porch.

Sometimes we'd eat slices of watermelon and have seed-spitting contests in the front yard. As cars passed by, we'd give a big, friendly wave, and some folks might stop and have a slice.

Homemade ice cream was a special Sunday afternoon treat. Wayne and I took turns cranking the handle of the ice cream churn round and round hundreds of times. As the milk, sugar, and flavoring mixed inside the metal cylinder and began to freeze, each turn became harder and harder. Our arms and shoulders ached in misery, but the thought of ice cream pushed us on, and we turned until we could turn no more. Mama would pack a towel around the top over the lid, and we waited long, anxious minutes for the cream to set. As payment for our cranking duty, Wayne and I huddled close by with spoons in hand, ready to scoop an extra bite as Daddy removed the paddle. Store-bought brands never stood a chance.

Some folks' front porches also doubled as informal concert sites, as locals brought their stringed instruments to play and sing bluegrass, country, and gospel. Those who didn't make music listened with toes tapping and hands clapping to the rhythm of a six-string guitar (pronounced GIT-tar), a five-string banjo (pronounced BAN-jer), and a four-string violin (pronounced FID-dle).

After the pickin' and singin' as friends and neighbors were fixin' to go home, the polite thing to say was, "Y'all come 'n go with us."

Every generation romances about the "good ol days" and those were some mighty good times. That being said, I'll take all of today's modern conveniences. The advances in technology make present-day living mighty good as well. But one summer evening, I'd love to go back to that time and place of front porch gatherings with pickin' and singin', watermelons and seed spittin'. Let me take another turn at the crank on the old-fashioned churn, and give me just one more giant-sized bowl of homemade ice cream.

If I could travel back to 1955 as Marty McFly did in the movie *Back to the Future*, if I could go back to that sweet, sublime, simple place and time once more, it's likely I'd say, "Y'all come 'n go with us."

Would we go?

Would we ever return?

Game of chance

**Siblings and cousins with
Pa and Granny Dottry in background.
L to R, first row: Jo, me, Nant, Diane.
L to R, second row: Larry, Glenn, Terry, Wayne.**

R ed Rover. Hop Scotch. Hide 'n Seek. Simon Says.
These and other childhood games were the ones we played
while growing up. They were held together by tradition and
a set of rules that were handed down from one generation to the next.
They were fun, and we remember them.

But there were also those spontaneous no-name games with no
pre-set rules, and no form. They were born from the instant reactions
of a free flow of energy. Those games instinctively burst forth with
imagination and no restraints. They were games of joy and laughter.
You forget how you played them, but you remember the feelings of
euphoria, and that stays with you for the rest of your life.

Our first cousins, Wanda and Diane, were visiting Nant one
summer evening. All three were close in age, between nine and ten

years old. Although they didn't see each other that often, there was a kindred bond among them. When the cousins came to visit, they'd hole up in Nant's room for what seemed like a girls' giggling contest. And that evening, when they'd giggled so much their sides could take no more, Wanda, Diane, and Nant burst from the bedroom door, through the kitchen and dining room, and onto the front porch.

Our front porch sat up from the ground about a foot high, so they started a sort of stepping-in-place-from-the-ground-to-the-porch kind of game. One of those spontaneous, no tradition, no rules games.

"I bet I can jump longer than you!" Wanda said.

"No you can't." Diane said.

Nant was having the time of her life playing with her best friends/cousins. Although I couldn't express it with adult words, as a kid I saw Nant's personality come alive as never before. On her face was an expression of pure bliss. Her long, dark hair bounced in rhythm as she played their high-step game free of reservation, reticence, self-doubt, self-consciousness, and inhibition. I had never, ever seen her so happy.

"I can jump all night!" Nant said with the confidence of an Olympic athlete, as she pulled her dress up to just above her knees for easier jumping.

Just at that moment, Daddy came through the front door and onto the porch. Nant's face fell, and I saw the dread in her eyes as she glanced over to him.

Without one word as to why, Daddy jerked Nant by the arm, and then slapped her four or five times on the face. Poor Nant, totally humiliated, crumbled into a rocking chair, sobbing with her face in her hands. Still without a single word, and with no explanation as to why he had "disciplined" Nant, Daddy strolled back into the house.

The little jumping game was over. No more fun, only heartbreak as Daddy brought it to an abrupt and embarrassing end. In a matter of seconds, I saw my sister's spirit entirely crushed. And for what?!? Because she was showing her knees?!?

I felt so sorry for Nant. My deep pity for her was matched only by the rage and disgust I felt toward Daddy. I hated him for what he did, but what could I do? I was an eight-year-old kid. I was helpless.

Although it's been nearly sixty years, that disgraceful memory is still vivid in my mind. Until recently, I had never spoken to anyone about that evening, not even to Nant. I suppose some memories are so distasteful we'd rather not speak or think of them.

Recently, Suzy and I were driving to an outdoor festival in South Pittsburg, Tennessee. As always, I had asked her to read portions of my stories for reactions and suggestions.

Nant

"These are good. Are there more stories from your childhood?" she asked.

With no warning, Nant's little jumping story bubbled up and burst out. All those emotions of pity, disgust, and anger gushed from within me like a waterfall. I cried for my sweet, innocent sister and I cursed that self-righteous devil of a daddy.

For sixty years I rarely thought about it. I never talked about it. I had not intended to write about it.

But I did. I'm glad I did.

Paradise lost

D addy was obsessed with land ownership. He saw it as a status symbol, and was impressed with people who owned large amounts of property. He frequently mentioned names of men from his past and said with great admiration, "He shore had a lot 'o land." Anytime anyone had acreage to sell, if it was possible for Daddy to scrape together the money, he'd buy it. At times Mama questioned the need to continue land purchases, but Daddy's answer was always, "They ain't makin' no more land."

One of his purchases was a six-acre tract in the forks of the road, the same forks of the road one half mile from our home. Even as a boy, I loved that spot. To me it was six acres of paradise. The land stretched out and rose above and between the two roads. It had been part of the farm owned by Daddy's grandfather, and was covered in a thick carpet of grass with a huge magnolia tree near the top. Many times I've climbed all the way up just to take in the view. From that vantage point I could see the Blue Ridge mountain range in the distance, and below, my church, my grandparents' homes, and my home. As I looked down the road that led by the church, the words to the song, "Church in the Wildwood" came to mind:

There's a church in the valley by the wildwood;
No lovelier spot in the dale.
No place is so dear to my childhood
As the little brown church in the vale.
Come to the church by the wildwood
Oh, come to the church in the dale.
No spot is so dear to my childhood
As the little brown church in the dale.

In fairness, I have to say that Daddy knew that was my favorite piece of property, and he refused to sell it to anyone else. His way of keeping it in the family, I assume. In my mid-thirties I was able to buy that parcel from Daddy for a reasonable price. I felt good about the deal until the final closing in the lawyer's office. Without any advance notice, Daddy announced he'd put a "life estate" on the land. This meant that as long as he was alive, he technically still controlled the property and what could be done with it. I expressed surprise, but Daddy reasoned once the land was paid off, he'd remove the life estate.

When I mailed my final payment to Daddy, I enclosed a letter reminding him of the life estate, but he did nothing. Mama later explained to me that she had opened the envelope, but did not let Daddy see the letter because she knew it would make him mad. What could I do except wait for Daddy to get in a better mood? In time he did, and the life estate was eventually released.

Once I moved away from home to attend college, I never lived there again for any length of time. But twice each year when visiting family in Walhalla, I'd walk to the forks of the road, and then trek through the weeds, brush, and beggar lice to the top, and take in the view once more. I dreamed of building a home there worthy of the gracious landscape. Unfortunately, as time passed, it became apparent that, as the song "I Dreamed a Dream" says, there are dreams that can never be. After years of seeing my dream fade, I finally decided to sell the land. It was such a choice piece of property it sold quickly, and at a good price.

Another meeting in another lawyer's office, and in a matter of minutes, it was gone. I knew it was the right decision, and at the right time. But it still hurts when I remember the beauty of that place with all its memories.

Daddy was right. They ain't makin' no more land. And they sure won't make another piece of property like that one. My six acres in the forks of the road.

A box of crayons

My first grade picture

P a Deaton had serious heart trouble, and most of my memory of him is while he was bedfast. Anytime I was eating at Pa and Granny's, Pa would ask, "Need 'ne hep?" Meaning, do you need any help eating that? I took it as a joke, but I'll bet he'd have taken me up if I'd offered him a bite.

Ol' Pa sure knew how to eat a watermelon with his four grandsons, Glen, Larry, Wayne, and me. He'd say "Boys, go to the watermelon patch and pick us out a big 'un." Pa would cut it into four pieces, and as he handed each one of us a slice he'd say, "Boys, I don't want much. Just give me a little piece of yours." With his pocket knife, Pa would cut the heart, the middle, the sweetest part of the watermelon out of each of our pieces for himself. We thought he was so generous. He didn't even take a whole slice, just took a little piece of ours.

(I tried that trick on my grandsons, Spencer and Andy, but it backfired on me. "I don't like watermelon, Papa Tony." Don't like watermelon? These kids today. What you gonna do?)

Pa Deaton died at age sixty-two, five years younger than the age I am now. I was six years old, and I have no memory of his death. To shelter me from the grief and drama of the funeral, I was farmed out to church members, Gene and Geraldine Addis. That was when I spent the night with my friend Ken Addis, and we rolled the wheel across his living room floor the next morning before going to church.

Daddy said the day after Pa's funeral, he and I walked to town so he could enroll me in school for the following fall. I never understood why we walked. Maybe our car wouldn't start. Maybe it was out of gas. I don't know, but good Lord, it was about seven miles each way. That was in April, 1955. I started first grade the following September.

We lived in the Keowee School District and should have attended the Keowee County School. But Daddy had a falling out with the school principal, Mr. Nalley, over the recent hiring of a fifth-grade teacher who was a Yankee. It was rumored that this woman from north of the Mason-Dixon line had bobbed-off, bleached-blonde hair, wore rouge and lipstick, and had the reputation of a street walker. Mr. Nalley tried to explain that the teacher had already signed a contract and was due to start teaching in the fall. There was nothing he could do, even if he wanted to.

"I don't care," Daddy argued. "That ain't the kind o' example I want for my girls, and she ain't teachin' my kids!" He stormed out of the principal's office and went directly to Mr. Stoudemire, the area school superintendent, with an appeal for us to attend school in town.

After a lengthy discussion, Mr. Stoudemire agreed. But he explained to Daddy that the school bus route ended at the forks of the road, and that's where his children would have to meet the bus. No matter; once Daddy got hold of a grudge he held on for dear life, and no kid of his was going to attend a school with a Yankee Jezebel teacher. As a result, rain or shine, hot or cold, like it or not, every day of the school year Wayne, Jo, Nant, and I made the half-mile hike to the forks of the road to catch the bus.

Mrs. Waldt was my first-grade teacher, and she was pretty good. I don't remember her being mean to me or any of the other children. On the first day of school she read us a story about a boy who, when walking to school on his first day, came to a fork in the road. Instead of following the road that led to school, the boy went the other direction and as a result, he didn't get along too well in life. When the boy became an adult he realized he had made a big mistake and had to start all over again in the first grade. Mrs. Waldt said by then he was so big a part of the desk had to be sawed away to make room for his knees when he sat.

Charlie Morgan and I became best friends from the first day of school, and we remained best friends throughout high school. I only see Charlie once about every five years at our high school class reunion, but to this day I still think of him as a close friend.

In first grade I learned the alphabet, numbers, and I read about Dick, Jane, and Sally. I also learned the different colors. Funny, but I still remember the first time I was introduced to the color purple. Guess I'd never seen purple before, and I thought it was the prettiest color I'd ever seen.

Most of the kids in my class had the Crayola brand of crayons neatly packed away in their school book satchels. I didn't have Crayola brand crayons, and I sure as heck didn't have a book satchel. An eight pack of Crayolas cost a dime, but there was another cheaper brand that only cost a nickel per pack. Crayolets. Guess which ones I had?

That was the one time I thought Mrs. Waldt was a little insensitive.

After seeing that I had the cheap, nickel-a-pack Crayolets, she held up my box beside another student's box of Crayolas and compared the two by pointing out the superior qualities of the Crayola brand and the inferior qualities of my crayon box. "Crayolets are waxy," she said. You'd have thought she was making a TV commercial for Crayola. I was quite embarrassed. I didn't need to be reminded in front of the whole class that I was poor. Well— that's how I felt, anyway.

About a week later, a student came to class with a box of 64 Crayolas complete with the crayon sharpener on the back. He beamed as everyone crowded around, admiring his trophy box and pointing out all the different colors. "And there's a purple!" I said. He didn't say anything, but looked up at me with a frown as if to say, "You're not invited to this party. You're not a Crayola. You're a Crayolet." The class system starts in early childhood.

In the room next to our class was a second-grade teacher, Mrs. Schumacher. She was a very pretty woman with striking features, a trim figure, and she carried herself like a model, but she had the hint of a mustache. With our woeful lack of social graces, she was constantly asked when she was going to shave her mustache. It must have been humiliating, but first-graders will be first-graders. Suffice to say the insensitivity Mrs. Waldt showed to me about the crayons never registered in my young mind when I joined the crowd asking about Mrs. Schumacher's mustache. Yep. First-graders will be first-graders.

I reckon I did OK in first grade. On the last day of the year when we were given our report cards, on them were typed either "Promoted" or "Not Promoted." I didn't even look at my report card, but when I met Wayne at the school bus, he told me it said "Promoted." I remember asking, "Are you sure it says, 'Promoted?'"

It did.

My first school, now the civic auditorium

Shall we dance?

M y second grade teacher was Mrs. Rochester, a sweet, humble woman. I always felt safe and loved around her. The second grade didn't start out well, though. That's the year the new Pine Street School opened. Wayne, Jo, Nant, and most of the friends I'd made in the first grade, including Charlie Morgan, were still assigned to the old school. But not me. I was assigned to the Pine Street School.

Unlike some kids' parents, Mama was not available to accompany me on the first day of school. She must have known I'd be a little scared or lonesome, and she had Wayne try to cheer me up. I was OK and hadn't thought that much about being by myself, but as the bus pulled up in front of the new Pine Street School, Wayne came to my seat and said, "Look at all 'em swing sets! You're gonna have fun!"

That's when it hit me. I knew I'd be alone. I don't know when I'd ever felt more lonely and scared.

It's kind of embarrassing to admit now, but a sudden wave of terror and helplessness swept over me as I walked into the auditorium, and I burst into tears. I cried and cried.

Eventually I saw a woman who looked familiar. I think she was distant kin on Mama's side. Maybe I'd seen her when visiting Cherry Hill Church of God. At least it was a face I recognized.

She didn't exactly open her arms to me, but I lingered near her until the class rolls were read and we all went to our classrooms. The kindness in Mrs. Rochester's face was apparent. She welcomed me and all the second graders to her classroom with genuine affection, and after a while I was fine.

I've never told anyone about this episode of fear and loneliness, not even anyone in my family. But I never forgot that day.

By contrast, an incident that happened in the second grade is a highlight of my elementary school years.

One morning our class met in the auditorium for a recreational folk dance. We were to pair up, girl and boy. Annie Bailes, who was

With Annie at a class reunion

the prettiest and most popular girl in our class, knew the dance and was going to teach it to the rest of us, but she had to have a partner to properly demonstrate how we were to dance. And who do you reckon she picked? Me! Me, out of all the other boys! Could she have thought I was cute?

To this day, every time I see Annie, she and I laugh about that. I wonder if she can imagine what a boost this was to my young, tender ego. I wish every child had a school memory this pleasant.

Unfortunately, my next memory from the second grade is anything but pleasant.

"Pa's dead"

Pa and Granny Dottry

"Heeeere guinea, guinea, guinea, guinea, guinea. Heeeere guinea, guinea, guinea, guinea, guinea."

"What ya doin' Pa?"

As we walked home from the school bus stop, Wayne, Jo, Nant, and I heard Pa calling in his high pitched, sing-song voice.

"Tryin' to round up 'em guineas," Pa said with a hint of humor and frustration.

Pa and Granny had a flock of guineas that didn't take too well to their new home and kept wandering back to their old home, the Casson Place.

"Want me t'help ya look for 'em?" Wayne asked.

"Naw, y'all better git on home," Pa said. "Ya' Mama'll be lookin' for ya."

"Well, hope you find 'em, Pa. See ya. Say hey to Granny."

As we strolled down the road toward home, Pa's chorus faded in the distance, "Heeeere guinea, guinea, guinea, guinea, guinea. Heeeere guinea, guinea, guinea, guinea, guinea."

That's my last remembrance of Pa Dottry.

Pa was Mama's daddy, or to be formal about it, my maternal grandfather. But there were no such formal terms as "Grandfather" and "Grandmother" in our world. Simply and affectionately, they were "Pa Dottry" and "Granny Dottry."

Pa was as big as a giant with a gruff exterior. His ruddy, Irish complexion was made even brighter from a lifetime of farming cotton outdoors in the sun. Granny's gentle, sweet nature complemented Pa with her hugs and kisses. We could always count on her for a piece of peppermint candy.

I can still remember when Pa and Granny lived at the Casson Place. Seemed to me that big house had twenty rooms. Granny kept the yard swept clean with a broom she had made from the branch of a maple tree. They had no running water, so after coming in from the field, Pa would hitch up the wooden sled to his horse, Trigger. I'd sit on the sled with a huge foot tub, and the three of us would head down to the spring. Boy that was fun! When we returned from the spring, Pa would sit on the back porch and soak his tired feet in the big tub. The dusty red clay he had worked in all day turned the water as red as a beet. I'd giggle, and ol' Pa would just grin and say, "That comes from hard work, boy."

I was eight years old when Pa died. It was November 28, 1957. Thanksgiving Day. Opening day of rabbit season.

Throughout the South, Thanksgiving Day is not only the holiday when Americans give thanks, and not only the beginning of

Christmas season; it's the day men and boys big enough to tote a shotgun wait for all year. As soon as the sun peeps above the eastern horizon, the countryside echoes with the booming of twelve-gauge Winchesters and Remingtons. Barking beagles are already in hot pursuit as poor ol' Peter Rabbit is having the worst day of his life. Talk about "a bad hare day!"

Pa and his son Grady, our uncle, had made plans to go hunting. Grady worked at the fiberglass plant in Anderson, but because it was Thanksgiving, he had a holiday.

Grady had the day off, but it was just another work day for his wife Helen, and also for Mama and her sister, Millie. They worked at the J. P. Stevens mill in Utica, South Carolina. Mr. J. P., in his wisdom, believed his employees should put in a full workday instead of enjoying time with family—a strain on the quality of mercy, if I do say so. As planned, however, Grady arrived at Pa and Granny's early that Thanksgiving morning ready to go hunting.

Grady should have barely stepped from his cherished "Forty Ford" sedan before hearing Pa bellow out, "Hey boy! Let's go get 'em!"

Instead, Grady was greeted with his father's big, rugged frame bent double as he paced the floor of his and Granny's four-room house.

With every step, both Pa and Granny were praying as hard as they could, asking for relief from the sharp pains in Pa's chest. Grady begged Pa to go to the doctor, but he would have none of it. Pa's trust was in The Great Physician, the God he had read about in his King James Version Bible. He was a man of deep faith. He lived by faith, and if God was to call him home, he would die by faith.

As fervent as Pa and Granny's prayers were, the chest pains worsened by the minute. Grady's repeated pleas for medical attention fell on deaf ears. He was getting scared, so scared he was convinced that without a miracle, the end was near.

Since Pa wouldn't allow him to send for the doctor, Grady went to the parsonage to ask Preacher Childers to come and pray. But, of course, Preacher Childers had gone rabbit hunting. Grady then drove to the home of a church member, Clint Bottoms, who lived down the road past our house.

"I'm comin' just as fast as I can, prayin' in th'name o' Jesus!" Brother Bottoms assured Grady.

After seeing Brother Bottoms, Grady stopped at our house to make Daddy aware of the situation. When he appeared on our front porch, Grady was visibly trembling. In a halting voice, he relayed Pa's condition and cautioned Daddy that if Mama was to see Pa before he died, she'd better come quickly.

We didn't have a phone, so Daddy drove to a neighbor's house to call Mama at work and give her the message. "Y'all stay here. I'm goin' to Pa and Granny's," Wayne said to Jo, Nant, and me. We knew Wayne would deliver the news, good or bad, as soon as he knew something.

After about an hour of looking, wondering, and worrying, we spotted Wayne returning from Pa and Granny's. Although he was way down the road near the end of the pasture fence, we couldn't wait, so we ran to meet him.

"Wayne! Wayne!"

But there was no response.

Catching our breath, we yelled again, "Wayne! What happened? Is Pa all right?"

As we drew closer, we saw Wayne's sad face. With big tears rolling down his cheeks, all he said was, "Pa's dead."

In stunned silence, the four of us walked back to Pa and Granny's.

Speed limits and traffic laws meant nothing to Mama, Millie, and Helen as they tore through the back roads of Oconee County.

Racing, hoping, and praying to find Pa alive.

Racing, hoping, and praying to say "I love you" just once more.

Racing, hoping, and praying to say a final "good bye."

After what must have seemed an eternity, Mama, Millie, and Helen finally arrived at Pa and Granny's. Pa lived just long enough for Mama to see him take a few short breaths as she kissed him and gently caressed his cheeks. Then he was gone.

That was my first experience with death and the grief that followed.

I'd never known anyone to cry and wail the way Granny did. She was inconsolable. Just one day before, Pa was full of life, raring to go rabbit hunting. Now, without warning, Pa lay dead and cold on the bed he and Granny had shared for more than forty years.

Granny told Preacher Childers, who by now had arrived, she was afraid the Holy Ghost had left her. Preacher Childers assured her that the Holy Ghost was with her now more than ever. But Granny found little comfort in Preacher Childers' well-intentioned words. She had lost the one she loved most. She was losing her mind. She was losing her faith. Granny was so sick with grief she was put to bed and remained there until the day of the funeral.

While I admire Pa's unrelenting faith, his faith may very well have caused his death. No one will ever know if Pa would have lived longer if he had been willing to be treated by medical professionals. One thing for sure is that a much loved husband, father, grandfather, brother, and friend died that Thanksgiving Day.

Faith is a powerful thing, but blind or misdirected faith can have disastrous consequences. I believe God is almighty and miraculous, but I also believe He uses doctors and medical science to perform what some may call miracles. It tempts me to say, "Pa, would it have been so wrong for you to go to the doctor? If so, maybe we would have had you for several more years. But you died that day."

Davenport Funeral Home was immediately notified. As was the rural custom, a local funeral business would take the deceased, prepare and dress the body, place it in a casket, and then return it to the home. Our Aunt Millie and her husband Melvin had recently built a nice brick rancher just down the road from Pa and Granny's. Since Pa and Granny's house was so small, it was decided that Pa would lay a corpse (the country term for lie in state) at Millie and Melvin's.

As word of Pa's death spread, Millie and Melvin's house filled with friends and relatives from near and far. I met kinfolks I never knew existed. Among them were Pa's brother, Uncle Dick, and Pa's sister, Aunt Mary, both from Elberton, Georgia. When I saw Aunt Mary, I thought she must be at least a hundred years old. She was the frailest woman I'd ever seen. Her face was all sunk in, and her cheek bones stuck out.

I asked Mama, "How old is she?"

I was shocked at Mama's answer: "About as old as Daddy."

As old as Daddy?! Naturally, I thought she meant Daddy—my Daddy. Then Mama explained, she meant her Daddy—Pa. But no way did I think Pa looked as old as Aunt Mary.

Still they came. Friends and family members were first greeted with smiles, hugs and light laughter, followed by a hushed, "I shore am sorry. We're gonna miss him." With drawn faces and furrowed brows, they made their way to Pa's casket. "Oh, don't he look good," came the familiar response.

I guess he did look good. He sure looked different. I'd never seen Pa in anything but bib overalls and a work shirt. But there he was all clean-shaven, hair neatly combed, and dressed in a blue suit, starched white shirt, and a red tie.

By Saturday morning, kind and generous church folks had brought in enough food to feed the Egyptian Army. Pa's funeral service was scheduled for Saturday at one o'clock, so at eleven o'clock the family gathered for a meal. After the meal, Preacher Childers said a prayer, and then Pa was loaded into the hearse while Mama, Daddy, Wayne, Jo, Nant, and I were directed to the "family car." When I sank down in that plush, limousine-style Cadillac, I thought man, this is nice!

Everyone stood in reverence to the deceased as Pa's casket was rolled down the center aisle of the Walhalla Number Two Church of God's crowded sanctuary. Preacher Shealy, a former pastor, stood, motioned everyone to be seated, then offered a somber welcome and extended his condolences to the family.

As requested, Preacher Shealy read from the Twenty-Third Psalm:

Yea though I walk through the valley of the shadow of death,
I will fear no evil, for Thou art with me.
Thy rod and Thy staff, they comfort me....
Surely goodness and mercy shall follow me all the days of my life,
And I will dwell in the house of the Lord forever.

The congregation then sang, "Farther along we'll know all about it..."

Although Daddy still held a bitter grudge toward Preacher Dillingham from 1951 for his action in having Daddy turned out of the church, Pa and Granny held the former pastor in high esteem, and Granny wanted him to speak at Pa's funeral. There was nothing Daddy could do about it except rant and vent his anger to Mama, which is exactly what he did.

On the morning of the funeral, when Mama and Daddy were getting dressed to attend the service, Daddy exploded in a fit of outrage that Granny had asked Preacher Dillingham to participate, and in his most hateful, mocking voice, Daddy expressed his disgust.

On the saddest day of her life, he verbally assaulted Mama with repeated insults about something over which she had no control. My heart ached for Mama. I can still hear Daddy's spiteful voice. I was eight years old, but don't tell me a kid is unaware.

Preacher Dillingham spoke of Pa's character, devotion to God, and his love of church and family. This was followed by a choir of assembled volunteers who sang about a land where we'll never grow old.

Last to speak was Preacher Childers, who delivered a brief message on Christian faith, the kind of faith our Pa Dottry had lived throughout his life.

The Scripture, songs, words of remembrance, and exhortation only served as a prelude to the most dramatic part of the service, the viewing of the body.

The ritual was the same as always. Mr. Davenport removed the family wreath from the center of the casket, raised the lid, and gestured for the "flower girls" to begin the procession. Jo and Nant, along with Uncle Ben's daughters, Annette, Janet, and Dona Jean, served as flower girls who would take wreaths from the tall metal frames to Pa's burial site in the church cemetery.

As a swell of emotion enveloped the sanctuary, I was confused as my cousin Janet, the first to approach Pa's casket, immediately began crying. For the two evenings of Pa's wake, she and her sisters had laughed and talked with Jo and Nant as if it were a regular family get-together, but now she was crying. And then Annette,

Dona Jean, Jo, and Nant all cried as they passed by Pa's casket. As I stretched my neck to try and get a better view, with the innocence of an eight year old I wondered, "Why? Why are they crying?"

The atmosphere was charged as the methodical march continued, row by row. In orderly fashion, church and community members filed by to pay their respects.

Pa's closest kin occupied the front rows of the left side of the church and had the honor of final viewing. Grady and Helen, followed by Uncle Ben, Pa's other son and his wife, Aunt Olga, choked back tears as they lingered at the casket. Mama and Millie wept openly as Daddy and Melvin stood by, helpless to offer comfort. It was all Mama and Millie could do to pull themselves away from the daddy they would never see again.

After a painfully long wait, Granny, so weak she had to be assisted by Mr. Davenport, made the longest journey of her life. She touched Pa's big weathered hands, kissed his forehead, and with heartbreaking tenderness, spoke to Pa as if he were still alive.

Mr. Davenport was kind and patient, but after a time he led Granny back to her seat. Then with quiet dignity, he closed the casket.

Overwhelmed by the finality of the moment, Granny's voice trembled with emotion as she pleaded, "Can I see him just one more time?"

Mr. Davenport gently nodded and raised the coffin lid to allow Granny to look again, and for the last time, at the face she loved.

Granny stayed at Millie and Melvin's for several days, but later moved back into the little block house she and Pa had shared. Wayne and I took turns with Jo and Nant spending nights with her—a pattern that continued throughout our grammar school, junior high, and high school years.

On those nights Wayne and I stayed with Granny, we learned she had the gift of a great storyteller. Granny told stories about her father who fought in the Civil War and fathered nineteen children, she being the youngest. It was hard to believe, but because of the wide age difference and a turn-of-the-century, horse-and-buggy lifestyle, Granny had brothers and sisters she never met during her entire life.

Her real talent was telling ghost stories—seeing ghosts, hearing ghosts, talking to ghosts, ghosts talking back, chains rattling, pots and pans banging, mysterious footsteps, pale-colored horses at midnight in the light of a full moon with a headless rider. She scared me to death! As Granny spun her terrifying tales, I kept my eyes glued on her, afraid to look to the right or to the left for fear I'd see a ghost, or a headless person. Oh, to have had a tape recorder back then.

One of our favorite stories was a funny one about when she and Pa were courting. Pa was from Georgia, and he tended to talk loud. Granny's brother, Garfield, didn't like Pa, and he once told him, "You c'n take 'at loud talkin' back to Georgie." I don't know if Pa and Uncle Garfield ever got along or not, but Pa sure married Granny.

The "loud talkin'" bit lives on as a family joke to this day. When any one of us gets excited and starts talking loud, somebody is sure to say, "You c'n take 'at loud talkin' back to Georgie."

Little by little, Granny became more like her old self. Before long, we saw that familiar twinkle in her eye. She was laughing again.

Time moved on, but one thing was always the same.

The huge Farmer's Almanac calendar that hung over the stove in Granny's front room was never turned. The month remained November. The red-letter date remained the 28th. And the year was 1957.

Thanksgiving Day. Opening day of rabbit season.

Behind the French doors

For some, the thought of chestnuts roasting on an open fire conjures up memories of an idyllic Christmas. For me, I'll take peanuts parching on a Dearborn gas heater.

Beginning in mid-October, cast members for the church Christmas play met for practice every Tuesday night at seven o'clock. The pulpit, piano, and organ were moved to provide a stage on the platform between the altar and the choir loft. A heavy gauge wire was strung across the front of the stage from one side of the church to the other. Bed sheets sewn together and fitted with curtain hooks gave the illusion of a proper theatre.

The theme of the play varied from year to year. One year it might be set in the modern day, with a story about some Scrooge-like scoundrel who has an epiphanal experience, and then turns out to be a real-deal Christian and does good things. Another year we might go back in time to the first Christmas. Shepherds costumed in bandanas and leather-like flip flops are startled at the announcement of the Savior's birth, followed by bathrobe-clad wise men in slow procession down the center aisle of the church—their eyes fixed on a star-shaped light bulb. And in the center of the stage, Mary and Joseph hover near a feed trough where a plastic baby doll Jesus sleeps peacefully.

Wayne, Jo, Nant, and I were always eager to be involved, and most years at least one of us was given a character to portray, or assigned to help in some part of the production. Sometimes Mama and Daddy participated as well. So every Tuesday night at six thirty, we'd head to practice.

The church was heated by free-standing Dearborn gas units in each of the four corners of the sanctuary. The units were box-shaped, about three feet tall, with an inset where ceramic bricks stood side by side and radiated heat from the blue flames that burned behind them. A protective grill of horizontal metal slats was fixed across the front, and near the bottom of the inset, in front of the bricks, was a little shelf about four inches deep.

Never wanting to be without a handy snack, Wayne usually brought a bag of peanuts—he called them pinders—to play practice.

He'd place the peanuts on the shelf in front of the ceramic bricks, and after a few minutes the church was filled with the heavenly aroma of parched peanuts. Wayne was proud of his handiwork. His eyes lit up as he took the peanuts in his hands, blowing hard to cool the hulls. He'd crack one open, blow again, and with a swift toss, pop the nut in his mouth and chew the crunchy goodness. Then, in the spirit of Christmas, "Anybody want some parched pinders?"

Life was good on those Tuesday nights, and Christmas was on its way!

About ten days before Christmas a large, freshly-cut cedar tree was delivered and set up at the front of the church sanctuary. Wednesday night after prayer meeting was designated for all who wanted to help decorate the tree. Strings of green, red, blue, and white lights the size of cucumbers encircled the tall tree from top to bottom, with gold and silver ornaments as big as baseballs hanging from every limb. Toddlers, teenagers, parents, and grandparents threw boxes of glittering silver icicles on the tree until it looked as if it had been plucked from high in the Swiss Alps.

Play practicing and tree decorating were all in preparation for the most anticipated night of the year for our church: Christmas Eve, the night of the Christmas play and exchanging of gifts.

Our family joked about Santa Claus coming to town and "What 'cha want Santa to bring you this year?" but even as a small child, it was just that—a joke. There was an obvious prejudice against Saint Nick.

I remember standing on Main Street watching the Christmas parade with Mama when I was about five years old. First came the fire engine with its screaming siren, then the marching bands from Seneca, Westminster, and Walhalla High Schools, followed by men and women on horseback dressed in cowboy and cowgirl outfits. (It only took one year for the parade organizers to learn you don't put horses in front of marching bands. It's bad enough for ten-foot-wide floats, or beauty queens perched on the backs of convertibles, to drive through animal waste, but even the proudest parents will look away as their little Carolyn in her white, band-uniform shoes steps in ankle-deep horse manure as she marches by playing "Oh come let us adore Him.")

I held Mama's hand as we watched the fire engine, marching bands, floats, beauty queens, horses, and manure. Finally, here came Santa Claus, smiling, waving, and showering the street with peppermint candy, his sleigh pulled by Dasher, Dancer, Prancer, Vixen, Comet, Cupid, Donner, and Blitzen. It was a happy moment for me, but as soon as Santa passed, Mama looked at me and said in a dismissive tone, "You don't believe in him."

My joy was dashed in an instant. At five years old, I didn't "believe *in* him" or "*not* believe in him." More than anything, I was caught up in the atmosphere of the parade.

Of course I didn't say it then, because what does a five-year-old say to his mother when she tells you not to believe in Santa Claus? Did she think my soul would be doomed to eternal fire if, for that fleeting moment, I loved Santa as much as I loved Jesus?

I didn't understand then, and I don't understand now why the jolly ol' elf was not a welcome part of our family Christmas tradition. As a youngster, my intuition told me it had something to do with our strict religious beliefs. Compared to Jesus, Santa Claus was "of the world," and was nothing more than a myth fabricated on a set of lies.

The wonder of fantasy is one of a child's greatest gifts, but I guess my parents thought a little innocent make-believe was too risky. Such a thing could draw attention away from the true story of Christmas.

But the true story of Christmas? I'm not disputing scripture here; I'm only saying that in my five-year-old mind, how could I distinguish one truth from another? "Round yon virgin, mother and child..." I didn't even know what a virgin was. Although I'd never seen an angel, I was told one appeared to a band of shepherds, and then a heavenly choir sang "Glory to God in the highest" while suspended in mid-air. And what about the wise men who came from a far distance, yet at every nativity scene were right there on the same night of Jesus' birth, along with the shepherds, Mary, Joseph, and Baby Jesus?

A little innocent make-believe?

Every family has its own traditions. Ours just didn't include the jolly fat man in a red suit from the North Pole. Other than perhaps "religious reasons" I don't know what Mama and Daddy's rationale was. I can only assume that because they had little money, throughout the year they were unable to provide some of the things other children had—like Crayola crayons. But Christmas was the one time of the year they allowed themselves a little excess in buying gifts for their children. I came to reckon that in their minds, no one, not even Santa, was going to cheat them out of the pleasure of telling their kids, "These are your Christmas gifts from Mama and Daddy. *We* bought these for you."

I still remember that momentary letdown at the Christmas parade, but Santa or no Santa, as a child I have nothing but wonderful memories of Christmas. When I opened my gifts, I wasn't thinking about who gave them to me. Honestly, I didn't care. And nothing could have taken the place of that feeling I had, come Christmas Eve.

Finally, it's Christmas Eve!

All day long both local radio stations, WGOG in Walhalla and WSNW in Seneca, played Christmas music. Real Christmas music. Carols such as "Joy to the World," "O Little Town of Bethlehem," and "Hark! The Heard Angels Sing." Those songs that find that special place in your heart you've been saving just for Christmas. The songs that swell from within until you think your heart will burst with joy.

Every conversation with every person you know says, it's Christmas! All of heaven and nature sings, it's Christmas! The milk cow with her long moo says, it's Christmas! Laying hens cackle with elation, it's Christmas! The wind whistles in your ear, it's Christmas! From the pores of every object on earth, living or dead, emanate the joyful sound, it's Christmas! For a kid, the anticipation bordered on mania—good mania—the kind that would drive you crazy.

Since the Deaton household more or less dis-invited Santa to stop by for milk and cookies, it made no sense to wait until Christmas morning to open the gifts he didn't bring. That was OK with Wayne, Jo, Nant, and me because we were allowed to open our presents on Christmas Eve, after the church Christmas play. For that reason, Christmas Eve was the biggest day of the year for us.

You'd have thought it was "Pack a Pew Sunday" as our church hosted a standing room only multitude who came to see the annual Christmas production. The faces of all people young and old beamed with the bright luster of Christmas cheer. The spirit of Christmas permeated the wooden floor, the carpet, the windows, the walls, the lights, and the ceiling of our church. Underneath the big Christmas tree down front lay a mountain of boxes of all shapes and sizes, filled with gifts to and from aunts, uncles, cousins, grandparents, friends, Sunday school members, and Sunday school teachers.

After the preacher's welcome, he turned the evening over to Sister Bertha, who was in charge of the play.

"Tonight's play is titled, 'Bob and his Christmas Chickens.' The part of Bob will be played by..." And down the list she continued, naming every character. Then the bed-sheet curtains were parted to reveal a set consisting of a sofa, lamp, end table, and an over-stuffed chair—a living room fit for any home.

This year the play was a story of how Bob found the true meaning of Christmas in some of God's most humble creatures. In the final scene of the play, Bob delivered his lines like a pro: "...so on Christmas morning as I fed my flock with can after can after can of crushed corn, I yelled out to them at the top of my lungs, "Merry Christmas, chickens! Merry Christmas, chickens!"

Curtain. Applause. Bows.

"Now I'm going to ask the members of the play to hand out presents," Sister Bertha said. And then the pandemonium began. Cast members shouted names for identification, and the lucky recipients raised their hands and shouted, "Over here!"

Shelby Harvey.

Albert Loudermilk.

Drucilla Lipscomb.

Dean Long.

Brenda Addis.

The names continued until every gift was placed in the outstretched hands of its grateful owner.

After a degree of calm was restored, the preacher and his wife were asked to approach the front of the sanctuary where Brother Jim, clerk of the church, presented them with a check in the amount of one hundred dollars as a gift from the faithful and grateful members.

The most beautiful moment came just before leaving the sanctuary when, with no accompaniment, the entire church sang "Silent Night." It was the most rapturous sound in this world to me. Although the congregational chorus was predominately made up of untrained voices, I would take that blend of glorious tones over the Mormon Tabernacle Choir any time. After the final verse we repeated the first verse. And as the last words, *Sleep in heavenly peace, sleep in heavenly peace* drifted into silence, a sacred hush settled in our house of worship. For that brief moment, every person knew the spirit of the Baby Jesus was real and in our midst. Finally, the preacher said something like, "Thank you God for the gift of your son, Jesus," and then abruptly shouted out, "Merry Christmas and good night!"

By now, I was a mix of hurry up and wait. I was anxious to get home to open my gifts, yet I wanted to cling to that moment, that feeling of sensational suspense. As we exited the doors of the church, everyone received a fruit bag—a brown paper sack filled with an apple, orange, tangerine, walnuts, pecans, Brazil nuts, a pack of Juicy Fruit chewing gum, and a Baby Ruth candy bar. The fruit, nuts, and chewing gum lasted till the day after Christmas, but the Baby Ruth didn't make it beyond the church parking lot.

Once we were home, Wayne, Jo, Nant, and I bolted from the car, through the front door, and into the living room where our treasures awaited. From year to year I remember gifts like dump trucks, cars, a battery-powered motor boat, a big red wagon, a cowboy outfit complete with cap pistols and fancy holsters, and an air rifle. Somehow Mama and Daddy always came through with the gifts we wanted.

Then there was one particular year when things were a little different. Wayne, Jo, Nant, and I always went on to church before Mama and Daddy, who stayed behind to set out our gifts. As usual, Mama had told each of us our presents would be in a specific place in the living room. Mine were to be in the green wingback chair next to the fireplace.

We rushed through the door, flipped on the light, and with pinpoint accuracy zoomed to our designated spot. In my chair was a box about eighteen inches by ten inches. I tore through the paper and ribbon and ripped open the box, only to find a blue and white plaid flannel shirt. Certain I had overlooked something, I looked at the chair again, around the chair, and under the chair. Nothing. I looked around the room to Wayne, Jo, and Nant who hadn't fared any better than me. Clothes!?

Then Daddy said to Wayne and me, "Boys, go get some wood so we can build a fire in the fireplace." Wayne and I were both thinking "this is the worst Christmas ever, and to make it even worse, we gotta go outside and haul in wood." As we pushed through the French doors from the living room into the dining room...

WHOA!

There stood four brand new Western Flyer bicycles.

Daddy laughed and said, "Just forget about that firewood, boys." And we did.

We couldn't believe it. Although we'd always gotten nice gifts, I thought only rich kids got bicycles for Christmas. But there they were—four of them, one for each of us—our names neatly lettered on a card and hung with a ribbon around the handlebars of each bike. Wayne's and mine were red, and Jo's and Nant's were blue.

That plaid flannel shirt didn't look so bad now. A single gift of clothing was a small sacrifice for a red, twenty-four-inch Western Flyer bicycle.

No, there was no Santa in our Christmas, but I can't imagine how it could have been better. A new bike, a plaid shirt, other gifts, fruit bags, Christmas tree decorations, play practice.

And peanuts parching on a Dearborn gas heater.

Ride 'em cowboy

I'd never ridden a bike, and Daddy didn't pay the two dollars extra for training wheels, so I had a learning curve to overcome. With the temperament of an army drill sergeant, Daddy barked, "When you start to fall, just turn the handlebars in that direction!" It took a while, but after some crashes, scrapes, skins, and bruises, I was riding my red Western Flyer from our house all the way to the forks of the road.

Wayne, about fifth grade

Some boys tried to make their bikes look and sound like motorcycles, with colored streamers out the ends of the handlebars, fenders mounted over the front and back wheels, and covered with five or six reflectors. A baseball card clothes-pinned to the wheel frame made a convincing engine-like sound as the card fluttered between the spokes of the spinning tire.

Then there were those of us who grew up influenced by the cowboy and Indian culture. There were so many old west shows and movies on TV it was hard to not think and act like a cowboy, so instead of motorcycles, our bikes were our horses. My cousin Dennis named his bike Trigger, the same as Roy Rogers' horse. I didn't give my bike a horse's name, and I don't think Wayne did either, but I guess he thought of it as a horse because he started to ride it like one.

The cowboy shows featured shootouts, train robberies, and fist fights, but most entertaining of all were the trick riders. Cowboys would clutch the saddle knob and hang onto one side of their horse as it raced away. Some stood straight and tall in the stirrups and others did handstands on the saddle while riding in full gallop. But one of the most daring tricks was the quick side mount. The rider would run alongside his horse, then spring from the ground and land squarely on his butt in the middle of the saddle. I never saw one miss a single time, and they made it look so easy—so easy that Wayne decided to give it a try with his "horse."

You know what's coming, don't you? And it ain't pretty.

I had ridden all the way to Pa and Granny Dottry's and on my way home, just past the church, I saw Wayne's bike over in the ditch.

"Wayne, where' ya at?"

All I heard was a low whimper and a feeble groan. Then I spotted him lying on the ground over in the woods beneath a pine tree.

"What you doin' over there? What happened?"

Poor ol' Wayne, barely able to speak, explained how he tried the quick side mount trick. He ran alongside his bike, then sprang off the ground with the intention of his butt landing squarely in the middle of the saddle. Only problem was, he missed.

Remember that cross bar on boys' bikes that runs from below the handlebars and back to just beneath the seat? That's where Wayne landed. Only it wasn't his butt that landed first.

To this day, I still wince, tense, and suck in two liters of air when I think about it.

That was the last time Wayne ever tried that trick.

And who'd have ever thought he'd grow up to be a fine bass singer?

Cousin Dorothy

Mama with Jo and Nant at Cherokee Indian Reservation

When we were kids our vacations, like those of most families, were determined by how big a dent would be made in the pocketbook. A day trip across the mountains to the Cherokee Indian Reservation was a big deal until later, when we took longer trips. To help with expenses, Mama packed food for us to eat at roadside picnic areas. On one of our trips we stopped for dinner, and Mama unpacked a pone of homemade cornbread still warm from the oven. We laughed, but it was good. The motels we stayed in would definitely be considered "budget." All six of us crammed into one room, with air conditioning that rarely worked, made the nights hot and stuffy. But hey! We were on vacation!

Cars didn't have seat belts, car seats, or restraints of any kind, even for infants or toddlers. When I was little, Mama and Daddy sat in the front seat, Wayne, Jo, and Nant filled up the back seat, and I was placed behind the top of the back seat near the rear windshield. I slept comfortably until Daddy had to make a sudden stop; then I'd tumble over the top of Wayne, Jo, and Nant onto the floorboard. I'd cry. They'd laugh, and then put me back up on my perch where I'd sleep until the next sudden stop.

Daddy must have joined a vacation savings club at work, similar to a Christmas savings club where an employee has a certain amount deducted from his check each week and placed into an account for later use. However he did it, Daddy always managed to have enough money for a family trip.

We were not a "go to the beach" kind of family. We loved the mountains. I remember my confusion when I saw people working in their yards, doing everyday things, as we drove by homes in the beautiful North Carolina and Virginia high country. I wanted to say, "You ain't supposed to work here. This is vacationland."

Sometimes our travels had a broad sense of plan but little attention to detail, except they often took us near friends and kinfolks because there we could enjoy a visit as well as find free lodging. Mama's first cousin, Dorothy, lived in Roanoke, so what the heck? Without a letter, phone call, or any prior notice, we decided to visit Cousin Dorothy. There was just one problem: We didn't know *where* in Roanoke she lived. Daddy made a long distance call from Virginia to Dorothy's father, Uncle Jess, in South Carolina, to get Dorothy's phone number. In talking to Uncle Jess, Daddy learned that Dorothy didn't live in Roanoke. She lived in Hollins. Daddy thought we'd messed up until Uncle Jess explained that Hollins is as close to Roanoke as West Union is to Walhalla. You can hardly tell where one stops and the other starts.

Although it was getting dark, Dorothy was still at work when Daddy called her house for directions. Her fourteen-year-old daughter, Linda, whom none of us had ever laid eyes on, was at home with a younger sister. Daddy tried to explain to Linda who we were, and that it was OK to let us come to their house, but Linda was smart. She told Daddy he'd have to call back after she talked to her mother. A few minutes later Daddy called again and Linda said we could come, and then gave Daddy directions to their house. Linda let us in the front door, but she kept her distance from this family of six strangers whom she'd never met. Bless her heart. She must have been scared to death.

After about an hour, Dorothy arrived home and greeted us with typical kinfolk gladness and kindness. Family stories were passed back and forth until about nine o'clock. The elephant in the room had still not been acknowledged, but Daddy was a master at code talk. He said, "Well, we'd better head down the mountain toward home." (We were in Roanoke, Virginia. Home was Walhalla, South Carolina. About an eight-hour drive.) As expected, Dorothy said, "Why, you are not. You're gonna spend the night with us." So we did. I don't know where anybody else slept, but I slept on a pallet on the living room floor.

Dorothy was a gracious host. She prepared a delicious breakfast for us the next morning, and when we were ready, as Daddy said, to "head down the mountain toward home," Dorothy directed us to an amusement park, where I took my first ride on a roller coaster. It was called The Wild Cat.

I jumped in the front car of the roller coaster beside Nant. The Wild Cat started low, level, and calm but just ahead loomed a high mountain of track. With a sluggish chuck—chuck—chuck, up we went, so slow I thought the Wild Cat would stall before we reached the top. When it seemed she'd made her final chuck—chuck— chuck, there we were at the summit with nothing below but a steep, steep drop. Then WOOOOOAH! It was the scariest fun I'd ever had, so I rode it a second time.

I have thought many times about how inconsiderate it was for our family of six to suddenly show up at Dorothy's house, unannounced, from out of state, so late in the day. But that was our standard mode of operation. I still remember that look of awkward uncertainty on young Linda's face as she skirted the walls of their house, keeping her distance from the strangers who had invaded her home.

In 2015, I saw Linda at a family reunion but had no idea who she was. She was next to me in line as we inched our way down the buffet table, piling our plates high with fried chicken, potato salad, and green beans. After hearing me tell one of my cousins how pretty our drive had been from Tennessee to South Carolina, Linda said, "If you want to see some pretty sights, go to Roanoke."

"I've been to Roanoke, and you're right; it's beautiful," I said. "Are you from there?"

Our conversation continued, and as the pieces of the puzzle fell into place, I realized she was Dorothy's daughter—the same teenage Linda at home in Roanoke on that July night nearly sixty years earlier.

I apologized for the uneasiness we caused and the imposition on her and her family, but Linda just laughed. Together we relived the whole evening, detail by detail, as though it were a fond memory.

With enough fried chicken, potato salad, and green beans, a bad recollection turned into a good story.

One worth retelling.

Sixteen tons and a Brown Cow

I loved my third grade teacher, Mrs. Gillespie. She had a good sense of humor with a hint of mischief about her, and it was obvious she cared about her students.

Me in a hand-me-down sweater

Each of the individual classes of the elementary grades presented a little skit for the rest of the Pine Street Elementary School. Mrs. Gillespie chose a variety show featuring the talents of her class. Three boys and I practiced Tennessee Ernie Ford's popular song, "Sixteen Tons." We didn't have a name, but on the morning of our show, we were introduced as "The Tony Quartet." (I didn't know I was the star of our group, but I guess I was.) That evening I told Mama about my singing, and she asked what I sang. When I told her "Sixteen Tons," she looked at me as if I'd sold my soul to the devil. I didn't dare say I hadn't sold my soul to the devil, but I did owe my soul to the company store.

Mrs. Gillespie took our class to the John C. Calhoun Mansion in Clemson. In her own way, she let us know she had to fight with the principal to get permission for the field trip. Now I understand why she was determined to take us there. She might have known that was not only her final year of teaching, but also her final year of life. Mrs. Gillespie died the following summer. Nobody said anything. She was just no longer around. It sure seemed strange. I missed her, but there was never any explanation as to what had happened to her. We were left with our silent, unanswered questions.

If properly handled, I believe it's better to let kids deal with the loss of a teacher or friend. It's better than just never knowing.

My fourth grade picture
(Check out the hair)

I had Mrs. Whitmire in the fourth grade. I loved her, too. Once she came to our house to check on me and the family. Teachers used to make visits to observe the home life of their students. In my situation, she may have suspected abuse.

In both of the cases below, the cuts and bruises were the result of a dumb kid and were entirely innocent. Still, it's easy to see how they could have looked suspicious. Plus, Mrs. Whitmire may have noticed other things about me that hinted of abuse.

I once pulled a set of metal venetian blinds off its brackets, and the slats cut me across my face and forehead. Another time, I was at Granny Dottry's and—crazy like kids can be—I leaned forward into her stovepipe and it burned my lip. I clearly remember Mrs. Whitmire asking me with some concern, "How'd you get that burn?"

For our fourth-grade class skit we presented a play about our forefathers and the founding of America. I don't remember a single line I said, but I remember the funny-looking hat I wore. We performed our historical drama on a Friday morning as the weekly assembly feature. As a reward, we didn't have our regular lessons that afternoon. Instead, Mrs. Whitmire had ice cream delivered to our class. Everybody got a Brown Cow.

You don't forget things like that.

During my next school year, I heard a hilarious story about my Uncle Quentin. I have since learned that over generations this same story has been handed down by others in different versions, but my family claims it as authentic. As the old saying goes, it was "told for the truth," and it remains a family favorite to this day. I will tell it now as it was told to me.

"And Jeee-zus said!"

"**A**ND JEEE-ZUS SAID!...."
Uncle Quentin was hitting his stride. He proclaimed once again: "AND JEEEEE-ZUS SAID!...."

"A-man!" "Glory to God!" "Preach it, brother!" echoed from the congregation of believers.

Uncle Quentin was on fire. His soul stirred with fervent zeal as his forefinger shook and pointed toward heaven. His face was blood red, and his body trembled with white hot passion.

So, what did Jesus say?

Mesmerized followers edged forward on handmade wooden benches. With eager ears and hungry hearts, they waited for the proclamation that was to follow. Jesus said many great things which are recorded in the gospels, but Uncle Quentin was about to reveal one of Jesus' declarations heretofore unknown to Christian disciples.

But I'm getting ahead of myself...

I was only ten when Uncle Quentin died. He was Charles Quentin Deaton, my grandfather's brother. That made him my great uncle, but of course I referred to him as just "Uncle Quentin." My memory of him is faint, but the stories of his colorful personality serve as vivid reminders of why he was one of my favorite relatives.

Uncle Quentin was born in the late 1800s, on the Ides of March, which made an impression on me because I was also born on the Ides of March. He was the oldest of six siblings.

Poverty was no stranger to this household in the remote backwoods of Oconee County, South Carolina. Formal education had no seat at life's lean table of bare necessities. The "school of hard knocks" was the unforgiving authority, and no one bothered to ask the rhetorical question, "What good is schooling if you ain't got nothin' to eat?"

As an adult, Uncle Quentin settled in a home just off Flat Shoals Road. A curved gravel driveway with a gentle grade led down to the dirt yard surrounding the unpainted wood frame house, flanked by two massive oak trees whose long branches stretched across the gabled tin roof.

Though weather-worn, the home appeared comfortable in its rustic surroundings. Its stark exterior was matched by its spartan interior. The furnishings consisted of straight ladder-back chairs with seats made of handwoven strips of hickory bark. Plain walls and creaky floors greeted guests with a sobering, "This is how the other half lives." Austere, grim-faced ancestors in sepia-toned photographs seemed to say, "Life is hard here."

For country folks, farming was the primary occupation. A few acres of rocky ground became the threadbare lifeline for families such as Uncle Quentin's. He struggled to stay above the treacherous economic waterline, while drowning in gulps of debt and inflation. Frustration and humiliation continued an unforgiving march. It became apparent that The Golden Rule was, in reality, "Them that's got the gold makes the rules."

Religion flourishes on both sides of the altar during times of economic depression. There are those who need to believe something is better, and those who will deliver the message of a better life. Though he was a little rough around the edges, Uncle Quentin had no lack of confidence, and he knew he could captivate a congregation—especially one willing to pay for a message of hope.

His farming business had come to a virtual standstill as the economic waterline reached its highest mark. This was the Great Depression era of the 1930s, and he had a family to feed. So he accepted the "call to preach."

Uncle Quentin was a big, gregarious man with an over-abundance of personality. Thus, preaching would be no problem for him. Fornication, liquor, and love of money were sufficient sin topics for a month of Sundays. There was one minor problem, however.

Uncle Quentin had no—and I mean no—formal education. As the old saying goes, "He couldn't read his name in boxcar letters."

Although conventional schooling wasn't considered by holiness people as a prerequisite for a preacher of the gospel, the reading of Scripture could not be ignored. Nevertheless, Uncle Quentin was determined that a lack of education was no reason to shirk the call of God. So he made a career-changing decision.

Monroe (pronounced "MUN-ro"), a trusted and learned friend, would serve as Uncle Quentin's assistant in his public orations. A man of many talents, Monroe could not only read and write; he could also sing and pick a guitar. He would assume the role of both song leader and devoted follower, so devoted as to shadow Uncle Quentin as he "read" his text from a giant-print Bible.

It worked liked this: Uncle Quentin held the Bible high in his outstretched left hand. With the index finger of his right hand, he traced the chosen text as Monroe whispered the words, phrase by phrase. Then Uncle Quentin bellowed each phrase as if he were reading it himself. Their tag-team ministry of intellect and inspiration ran with clockwork precision. It was poetry in motion. Uncle Quentin became known as "a man o' God who could preach the gospel with the best of 'em."

Success was on the horizon.

Uncle Quentin's big break came when he was engaged by the Ryder Mountain Holiness Church to preach a brush arbor revival the first week of August. Opening night was scheduled for August 2. The searing sun had shown no mercy all day long, and the evening shadows brought little comfort. The air was thick and still as the congregation assembled. Only cardboard fans from Ansel's Funeral Home provided momentary relief from the oppressive heat and humidity.

"Turn in your hymnbooks to page 339 and let's sing 'I Shall Not Be Moved,'" Monroe called out.

This was followed by "A Little Talk with Jesus Makes it Right," and finally the favorite, "I'll Fly Away."

Refreshed by the rushing wind of the Spirit, everyone clapped as they sang with full voice, Iiiiii'll fly away, oh glory…

The mood was set. The atmosphere was charged with anticipation. Hearts and minds were in one accord as Uncle Quentin stepped forth to deliver the message of the hour.

Monroe took his assistant's position, prepared to execute the foolproof plan. With careful deliberation, Uncle Quentin opened his giant-print Bible to the predetermined page. The big, black Bible rested in the palm of his outstretched left hand, with the index finger of his right hand just below the selected reading.

"I shall take my text from Matthew 19, verses 24 through 26," Uncle Quentin declared with confident authority.

Monroe whispered, *"And I say unto you…,"*

"AND I SAY UNTO YOU…" Uncle Quentin repeated in a robust tone.

Again Monroe whispered, *"It is easier for a camel…"*

"IT IS EASIER FOR A CAMEL…"

"To go through the eye of a needle…"

"TO GO THROUGH THE EYE OF A NEEDLE…"

Their timing was impeccable. The routine continued in a seamless flow of perfect rhythm. Then came verse 26.

"And Jesus said…,"

"AND JEEE-ZUS SAID…,"

At that moment, the Bible slipped in Uncle Quentin's sweaty palm, causing his index finger to cover the next line of scripture.

"Move your fanger!" Monroe whispered under his breath.

"MOVE YOUR FANGER!" Uncle Quentin rang out with all his might.

At this point, the congregation was thinking, "Huh? Move your fanger?"

But Uncle Quentin was in his element, and he declared even louder: "AND JEEEE-ZUS SAID, MOOOOOVE YOUR FANGER!"

"Oh, you've played hell now!" Monroe admonished between his lips.

Still following Monroe's lead as if it were the very voice of God, Uncle Quentin could hardly contain his fervor. He announced his final proclamation with a fiendish revelry: "OHHHHHH, YOU'VE PLAYED HELL NOW!"

Instead of "A-man!" "Glory to God! "Preach it Brother!" an uneasy hush fell over the crowd of gathered believers. Uncle Quentin was taken aback by the reaction of his assembled flock, who were now making an awkward, hasty exit.

Oblivious to the situation, he struggled to recapture the moment. He leaned toward Monroe, listening for his cue, but all he could hear was the sharp "snap, snap, snap" of Monroe's guitar case.

Monroe asked incredulously, "And Jesus said, 'Move your fanger?'" Shaking his head as he walked away, "What the hell was you a'thankin'?"

Uncle Quentin was speechless. Alone now, all he could think of was what might have been. The dream of Reverend Quentin Ministries was over.

No tent.

No bus.

No offering.

Back to the cotton field.

Puppy love

"Chum here, buddy! Chum here!" I called in a falsetto voice to the little four-legged, six-week-old-puppy. He rambled over to my outstretched arms with a "Can I go home with you?" look all over him, and at that moment I knew he was the one.

Roger Duncan's bitch mutt (it's fun to say "bitch" and not be accused of swearing) had a litter of eight puppies, so he was eager to give away at least seven of them. Daddy was strict about a lot of things, but when it came to boys and puppies, I didn't even have to beg. Daddy understood an eleven-year-old boy needs a puppy, so he sent Wayne and me over to Roger's to pick mine out.

As I cradled him, I noticed speckles around his nose, mouth, and eyes. I had speckles around my nose, mouth, and eyes too. Mine were called freckles, so from the get-go I decided Freckles was a good name for my new puppy.

As soon as we were home, I fixed him a big bowl of milk with loaf bread crumbled inside, and set it on the side porch. Freckles lit into that bread and milk and lapped it up without a pause. "You know he's gotta stay outside," Daddy said. But that didn't matter. I made him a bed with an old blanket in the corner of the smoke house, and Freckles was right at home. He whimpered as I started to leave, so I stroked his head and down his tan-colored back, and again with my high-pitched voice I assured him, "It's OK. You'll be all right. I'll be back first thing in the morning. Good night, Freckles."

Freckles was my little buddy. He followed me everywhere, bouncing along full of fun and energy and with such a friendly personality, or as Wayne called it, a friendly puppy-ality. After school and on weekends we ran and played in the front yard, side yard, back yard, in the pasture, the hollers, and on the hillsides. Sometimes I'd lie down in the grass and Freckles would crawl all over me. I knew Freckles loved me, and I sure loved him.

Although it was a beautiful spring evening, I had homework to finish before me and Freckles could run and romp around in the yard. With my arithmetic book and Blue Horse notebook in my lap, I sat in the green and white metal glider on the front porch. Nant was helping me with long division homework. I was looking down, watching the number 7 vanish beneath Nant's impatient eraser.

"No, it's not 7!" she said, throwing up her hands in frustration. "It's a...."

Nant's voice stopped abruptly as we both heard the sudden screech of tires, followed by a high-pitched "Arp! Arp! Arp!"

I knew it was Freckles.

Freckles had been frolicking in the narrow strip of grass below the rock wall between our yard and the road. He was just getting old enough to chase cars, so when Daddy's first cousin Edward came racing by, naturally Freckles ran after him.

With no fence around our yard and no pets allowed in the house, it was not uncommon for us to return from town, church, or any short drive and find one of our cats or dogs lying in the middle of the road—killed by a passing vehicle. Fortunately, I didn't have to witness those horrible accidents. And although we were sad to know one of our pets had been killed, those were family pets.

This time it was different. It was my pet. My puppy. My Freckles.

Daddy and Wayne came running from the back yard as soon as they heard the screeching tires and Freckles' pitiful yelps. "I shore am sorry, Harris," Edward said, "He just run right out in front of me." But being sorry was no consolation. As Freckles continued his agonizing "Arp! Arp! Arp!" I held onto hope that maybe he was just hurt bad, and I could bandage him up and he'd be OK.

"Wayne, go get the baseball bat," Daddy said. I knew what was about to happen.

Edward told Daddy he shore was sorry, but nobody said "I shore am sorry" to me.

Nobody said, "Tony, go inside." (You shouldn't have to see this.)

Nobody said, "Freckles won't be in pain anymore."

Nobody said, "We'll get you another puppy, and you can name him Freckles."

Nobody said *anything* to me.

When Wayne returned, Daddy instructed him to hit Freckles on the back of the head. One more "Arp!" And then silence.

Freckles was dead. Killed right in front of my eyes.

Even my eleven-year-old mind knew it was a crude but necessary form of euthanasia—a mercy killing. Freckles was as good as dead the instant Edward's car struck him, and the blow by Wayne to the back of his head was only to relieve his suffering. Freckles had to be finished off, and the sooner the better, but that didn't keep nickel-sized tear drops from falling onto the pages of my arithmetic book and onto my long division homework. I was heartbroken. Nant didn't have the maturity or understanding to comfort me or try to ease my pain. And neither did anyone else try to ease the harrowing echoes of screeching tires, Freckles' cries for help, the dreadful sight of his lifeless body spinning on the asphalt like a rag doll as he was given his final death blow, and the sound of Freckles' final dying yelp.

I was too distraught to do anything. My insides were raging, but I sat still and powerless as I watched Daddy and Wayne grab my puppy by the tail and drag him away. I never knew where he was dumped or buried.

I was so blue I didn't smile for days, but there was not one kind or understanding word from anyone. It was as though it had never happened. Before leaving for school one morning, I said to Mama, "I'm so sad. I just can't get over Freckles."

I'm not sure how I thought Mama would respond. Maybe something like, "Oh, I understand. I miss him too. But can't you just see ol' Freckles in puppy heaven now. I'll bet he's running and playing all around the hills and hollers and having a big ol' time."

I don't know what her motive was or why she said what she did, but I sure didn't expect her stern, "You outta be ashamed of yourself for having so much feeling for a little ol' puppy."

I desperately needed consoling, but what I got was a cold-hearted scolding. I was so hurt and confused I didn't know what to think. An eleven-year-old boy isn't supposed to have feelings for his puppy? And this was from Mama, the person I could always turn to for tender love and compassion?

I guess feelings were supposed to be extended only to humans. Puppies didn't count.

Well, I'm sorry to disappoint you, Mama, but I had feelings then, and I have feelings now—for all of God creatures, both great and small—and I sure had feelings for "a little ol' puppy."

Fifty-six springs have come and gone since I was that fourth-grader who struggled with long division. I still get emotional—nickel-sized tears still flow—when I think about that awful evening in 1960, when I saw my fun-loving puppy with spots on his face killed before my eleven-year-old eyes.

My buddy. My puppy. My Freckles.

A fire and a fight

O ne early December morning when the temperature had plummeted to bitter cold, my siblings and I began our weekday sojourn up to the forks of the road.

Jo and Nant were bundled in wool kerchiefs, car coats, long dresses, and warm tights. Wayne and I thought it was sissy to overdo dressing in cold weather. A light jacket, flannel shirt, and a pair of overall britches were more than sufficient for us hardy country boys. Wayne never wore a cap because he didn't want to mess up his hair, and I always did whatever Big Brother did.

"I sure hope Granny Deaton gives me some mittens for Christmas," Nant said as we passed Granny's house. "My hands are freezing."

"Yeah, mine too," said Jo. "I just hope the bus is on time. We'll freeze to death if we have to wait for it."

Wayne and I walked on ahead of Jo and Nant. As we approached the parsonage, Wayne must have thought of Linda Sue Watkins, who attended our church. He took out his comb, and as he started to rake through his hair he came out with a big "Ouch!"

"What's the matter?"

"My hair's froze."

"Lemme see."

"No! Don't touch it. It'll break."

"Wayne's hair's froze!" I called back to Jo and Nant.

"You oughta wear a kerchief like me n' Jo," Nant said. "Then your hair wouldn't freeze." Jo and Nant giggled like girls giggle at brothers.

"Yeah, get yourself a kerchief, Pretty Boy," Jo mocked. And they giggled some more.

"Ha-Ha!" Wayne snorted sarcastically.

By the time we reached the forks, the four of us were so cold we could barely move. We waited and waited, but no bus.

"Wilburn must be driving today," Jo said. "He's always late."

"I'm gonna build a fire," Wayne said.

"What?" Jo asked.

"I'm gonna build a fire right here. Go get some straw."

Wayne never smoked—well, except when he and I and our cousins, Glenn and Larry, sneaked around and smoked rabbit tobacco leaves rolled up in newspaper—but to look cool, he carried a flip-top Zippo lighter in the watch pocket of his britches. We gathered arms of straw from the field where the road forked, bundled it, then placed it in a heap on the asphalt.

Wayne flipped open the top of his Zippo and with the sharp flick of his thumb, a flame shot forth. He cupped his hand around the precious glow, slowly knelt close to the yellow bundle, and set it ablaze. We relished in a momentary burst of warmth. But in a flash, it was over.

"Get some more straw," Wayne ordered.

But just as we ran toward the field, we heard the roar of the approaching bus. As we boarded, the pitiful remains of our open-air heater lay in full display for everyone to see.

"I've never seen anybody build a fire right in the middle of the road," Mary Todd said.

"It was so cold out there, Wayne's hair froze." Nant snickered.

The front of the bus was full, so Wayne, Jo, Nant, and I sat in seats across the aisle from each other near the rear. Billy Rogers, the school bus bully, swaggered back through the aisle with his eyes fixed on Wayne. Billy was older, bigger, and meaner than Wayne, and in a one-on-one fight Billy might have had the upper hand.

Like most siblings, we fought among ourselves, but if anyone else threatened one of us, we bonded with family allegiance. Nobody could get by with hurting one of us as long as the rest of us were around.

"Hey, Deaton! Ears cold?" Billy taunted. Then he thumped Wayne's left ear.

Wayne took a swing in defense, but before Billy had a chance to counter, Jo grabbed a handful of Billy's hair and was ready to snatch him baldheaded, while Nant sank her teeth into his arm like a mad bulldog. I, being the youngest and shortest, pounded the closest body part I could reach. Too bad for Billy, because his belly was just the right height for a punching bag, and I let him have it with both fists.

Students immediately gravitated to the back of the bus for a ringside seat. As fists, sweat, spit, blood, and curses sailed through the air, some hollered, "Hit 'im Wayne!" Others screeched, "Git 'im Billy!"

"Y'all stop that right now!" Wilburn yelled as he slammed on the brakes.

To Billy's good fortune, the sudden stop of the bus pitched him forward and he tumbled to the front of the bus.

"Now set down, ever' one o' you, and don't a one o' you git up again!" Wilburn commanded.

Wilburn was not one to be taken lightly. He'd been known to put troublemakers off the bus and make them walk to school. Nobody wanted to face the unforgiving elements, so everyone returned to their seats. Order was restored, and it was quiet.

"Huh!" Wilburn puffed in disgust, then took a check-glance in the rear-view mirror, put the bus into gear, and pulled forward. The low groan of the engine covered the momentary awkward silence. But after about a minute, whispers and mumbles were exchanged. Then Fred Brewer, who was not known to back down from a fight, gathered his nerve and mocked Billy in a loud voice.

"Hey Billy, why don't you go back and finish your fight?"

"Shut up, Brewer!"

"What's the matter, Billy? Can't you whup 'im?"

"If you fight one uv 'em, you gotta fight all four uv 'em," Billy huffed. "Why don't *you* go fight 'em, Fred?"

Fred did not take up the challenge.

No, thank you, Spiegel

I wonder what it's like out there, out there beyond them
*   mountains.*
Where the folks talk nice, an' the folks dress nice like y'see in
*   the mail order catalogs.*

From Carlisle Floyd's opera, *Susannah*

M y wife and I disagree about money. We don't disagree about how our money should be spent, but about what money can buy. She says money won't buy happiness, and I say it will. Comedian Archie Campbell's take was, "Money may not buy happiness, but it'll buy the best brand of misery you've ever seen." Whatever. I am generally a happy person, but if I had the money of Bill Gates or Warren Buffett, I can think of a lot of things I would buy and do for myself, my family, and for others that would make me even happier.

As noble as it may sound to some, growin' up pore ain't all it's cracked up to be. I hear stories of people who say, "We was pore, but we didn't know it 'cause everybody else was pore." That may be true for them, but not for me. I knew I was poor. It's not hard to figure that out when, on the first day of school, other boys are dressed in new shirts, pants, and shoes, and I'm wearing hand-me-downs. Sure, there were some families on the same economic scale as ours and some who were worse off, but with a family of six on a textile worker's income, we teetered pretty near the poverty line.

But wait. Help is on the way.

Maybe.

A Spiegel catalog unexpectedly appeared in our mailbox. It was beautiful. I suppose to some it was just a catalog, something to use in an outhouse, but to our family, it was a dream-come-true wish book. Pictures of children, adolescents, and adults neatly dressed in the current year's fashion covered the slick pages of the two-inch-thick book of fantasy. And tucked inside was an easy-to-complete application for mail order merchandise. I can still see the optimism in Mama's bright eyes when, with pen in hand, she confirmed a size eight pants for me. The "Send no money now / Easy monthly payment option" was too tempting, so Mama ordered clothes for the whole family.

With high hopes we waited for our new arrivals. But after four weeks of anticipation, instead of packages of shirts, pants, skirts, blouses, and dresses, the mailman delivered only an envelope from Spiegel.

Our credit application had been denied. No new clothes.

Daddy was a complex man with many sides, but when it came to finances, he was upright and reliable. He paid his bills and took pride in his credit record. When money was really tight, he'd go with cap in hand and plead for an extension on a loan. Even with the occasional extensions, he could borrow a sizeable amount of money with just his signature, because the local bank knew it could trust him. Whatever wording Spiegel used for its denial didn't matter. Our household income didn't meet their criteria. We weren't "one of them."

They were the Crayolas. We were the Crayolets.

Nobody explained to me why I wouldn't have a new pair of pants, because verbalizing the reason would have made it harder for Mama and Daddy. I sensed their helpless disappointment. I was disappointed too. So, like Susannah in Carlisle Floyd's opera, I wondered what it was like out there, where the folks dress nice like you see in the mail order catalogs.

Today I have a cedar closet full of suits, sport coats, pants, shirts, and two racks of silk ties. At last count, I have twenty-six pairs of shoes, eight pairs of boots, and four pairs of sandals. My wife says I have a sock fetish. Maybe I do, because I have three drawers full of socks (one with nothing but warm, wool socks; I remember how in winter months my feet were always cold).

And for "work clothes" I have three tuxedos, plus a complete set of white tie and tails.

Not one piece of my wardrobe, not even a pocket handkerchief, was ordered from a Spiegel catalog.

No, thank you, Spiegel. You can keep your snooty merchandise.

Ain't had so much fun since Uncle Quentin died

S o the question remains: Was he Uncle *Quentin*, Uncle *Quenten*, Uncle *Quenton*, or Uncle *Quention*?

The local newspaper printed his obituary as Charles Quenton Deaton, but his grave marker at Wolf Stake Baptist Church reads Charles Quention Deaton. Maybe the engraver was paid by the letter so he decided to add an "i" to help buy new shoes for his baby.

The fact that Uncle Quentin was illiterate might explain the different spellings of his name. Even he may not have known which spelling was correct. Since it seems I have a choice of spellings, I'll stick with *Quentin*.

Uncle Quentin and I share a birth date, March 15—the Ides of March. He died in 1959 at age sixty-six—one year younger than I am now. I hope this is not an omen; otherwise, I may never finish this memoir. Although I hardly knew him, I had heard the stories told of Uncle Quentin and his colorful character. His decision to preach, with its unfortunate results, is only one example of his charismatic personality.

Home telephones were not a common convenience when Uncle Quentin died, and it was long before email, Facebook, Instagram, Twitter, or any other social media. But when a death occurred in the community it was big news, and word spread in a matter of minutes. Suddenly, there was a refocus of priorities, and as folks gathered to offer support, it became a time of reacquainting and bonding with friends and family.

Two years earlier, I had observed a similar scene when Pa Dottry died, and I would see it again at Uncle Quentin's death—but in a very different way.

Uncle Quentin was survived by his widow, Helena, three sons, five daughters, one sister, one brother, and eight grandchildren. Everyone except his son Joel lived within a couple of hours' proximity to Walhalla. Only a week before Uncle Quentin's death, Joel, a career military man, had been reassigned to White Sands Missile Range in New Mexico and was given a few days' leave before reporting for duty. Meanwhile, his wife Lou had entered the hospital and given birth to a son.

Then came the startling news: Joel's father, Uncle Quentin, had died.

Despite the urgency of the moment, Joel could not leave his recently assigned base until every detail of military processing was complete.

My brother Wayne, also career military (now retired), explained to me that reprocessing involves quite a long list of paperwork. Among other things, the reassigned soldier must register in the offices of finance, medical, dental, and housing. He must also report to the company commander, the local probate judge, and be issued a new uniform.

Under the circumstances, the process was accelerated as much as possible, but in typical military protocol, every "i" must be dotted and every "t" crossed, resulting in a prolonged and tedious procedure. Once completed, Joel's next task was to have his wife and their newborn son released from the hospital. And then there was packing and preparing for a cross-country trip.

After completing every painstaking detail, Joel, Lou, their eight-year-old daughter Elaine, and their five-day-old son, Keith, began the long drive from New Mexico to South Carolina. Emotionally and physically exhausted, they left on a Tuesday morning, but by noon, another major hurdle: Joel became severely ill with stomach ulcers. Lou, still recovering from childbirth, placed her tiny son in a banana box and secured him in the front seat between her and Elaine, while Joel tried to find comfort stretched out in the back seat. Lou then took the wheel of their green and white '54 Oldsmobile, and continued east.

Back in Walhalla, Uncle Quentin's body had been taken to Ansel's Funeral Home, where it was prepared, dressed, placed in a bronze-colored casket, and then returned to his home on Flat Shoals Road. There was a push to have Uncle Quentin buried the next day, but his wife, Helena, insisted no final decision would be made until Joel and his family arrived. Therefore, the exact date of the funeral was "to be announced." Meanwhile, everyone began gathering for the wake.

As part of the family, Daddy felt obliged that we participate in the wake with the other relatives. When we arrived the first evening, I expected an atmosphere of gloom similar to what I had seen two years earlier when Pa Dottry died—long-faced mourners sitting in quiet respect for the dead. But the mood was quite the opposite. Even before we entered the house, we heard boisterous laughter echoing from within. Uncle Quentin's house was filled to overflowing with relatives and countless friends who had come to "mourn" the loss. I'd never seen grief expressed this way, but to be honest, it was a welcome change.

Mounds of fried chicken, ham, potato salad, green beans, macaroni and cheese, and casseroles, casseroles, casseroles, not to mention cakes, pies, and cobblers, topped the kitchen table and every available surface. I guess Mama knew there would be plenty of food, because we didn't have our usual bowl of beans, cornbread, and buttermilk for supper before we left home. I loaded my plate with two drumsticks, a huge helping of macaroni and cheese, a piece of German chocolate cake, and a big spoonful of peach cobbler. I expected Mama to make me eat some green beans, but she just looked at my plate, then at me, and smiled.

After they were well fed, some of the men gravitated outdoors for more spirited conversations. Daddy stayed inside to pontificate his views on religion and politics, but Wayne and I went out to be "one of the boys." As the smoke of Chesterfields and Camels swirled around tree branches, we got a first-hand education in blue collar man-time. There was an endless string of hunting and fishing tales, war stories, outright lies, and jokes about men and women having sex. I didn't always get the punch line to the jokes, but I laughed as if I did.

It didn't take Wayne and me long to figure out that "be right back" meant a quick trip to the car for a swig of cheap likker. We were growing up fast, and we liked it.

Meanwhile, across the plains of Texas, Lou continued the drive while tending to a sick husband, an eight-year-old daughter, and an infant son. From Texas, then Louisiana, Mississippi, Alabama, and into Georgia they continued. After two long days the journey's end was in sight, so late Wednesday afternoon Joel phoned ahead to say, "We'll get there sometime tomorrow."

With the anticipation of Joel's arrival, the Wednesday night wake crowd was more raucous than before. Not wanting to miss another opportunity for free food and entertainment, we stayed really late that night (so late, in fact, that Mama said we could stay home from school the next day). Outside, the hunting and fishing tales, war stories, lies, and jokes got bigger and bigger as the swigs of likker became more and more frequent. Oblivious to Daddy, Wayne and I now felt fully accepted as members of the "Blue Collar Man-Time Club," but we stayed away from the likker.

I laughed more and learned more on those two nights than I'd laughed or learned in my lifetime. I could hardly wait to get back to school so I could tell my buddy, Ralph Winkler, the stuff I'd heard.

On Thursday afternoon, completely drained of energy and with raw emotions, Joel, Lou, Elaine, and Keith arrived safely. Last-minute arrangements were made and the funeral was scheduled for Friday. Mama kept us out of school again so we could attend.

The service was held at Wolf Stake Baptist Church at noon, and was attended by a crowd of friends and relatives. The procedure was similar to the other funerals of that time. There were comments about the deceased and singing of hymns. I thought "There is a Fountain Filled With Blood" was about the most depressing thing I'd ever heard. The idea of a fountain gushing with blood also seemed pretty gross. I still find the music gloomy, and the idea of being plunged beneath a flood of blood, except in the most figurative sense, is something I will avoid at all cost. That being said, now in my mid-sixties I think of death quite often, and I take comfort in the words of William Cowper, as found in the final verse of this hymn:

When this poor lisping, stammering tongue
Lies silent in the grave;
Then in a nobler, sweeter song,
I'll sing Thy power to save.

Finally, there was the viewing of the body. I remember the sad and helpless look on the face of Uncle Quentin's youngest son, Bill, only fifteen years old, as he gazed down at his dead father.

On Monday morning when I entered my fourth-grade classroom, Mrs. Whitmire called me to her desk and said, "I'm very sorry about your uncle."

"Ma'am?"

"Your uncle. I'm sorry for your loss."

"Yes ma'am. Thank you."

When I sat down at my desk behind my friend Ralph, he turned and asked. "Where ya been?"

"Tell ya later. But I ain't never had so much fun in my life."

Student teacher

W hat are the odds in such a small town? In fifth grade, I encountered yet another Mrs. Whitmire. She was the sister-in-law of my fourth-grade Mrs. Whitmire. But she was a completely different person.

I hate to say it, but she was mean. All of the kids in her class were scared to death of her. Even Annie Bailes, who I thought was the teacher's pet, was afraid of her.

This Mrs. Whitmire would not hesitate to strike a student across the back with her quarter-inch-thick yardstick. I did misbehave from time to time, but once I was sitting at my desk not doing a thing. Mrs. Whitmire was on one of her routine patrols between the rows of desks when, out of nowhere, she flailed me across the shoulders.

"I wudden doin' nothin'!" I protested.

"Yes you were," she said, "and if you say another word, I'll hit you again."

I kept quiet.

One positive thing I remember and appreciate about Mrs. Whitmire was her love and knowledge of Civil War history and the music of that period. With her set of vinyl records and a portable record player, she spent an hour a day for a whole week reading historical excerpts and playing Civil War melodies. The class was close to tears as she explained that the song "Somebody's Darling" was about a young soldier, probably no more than fifteen or sixteen, who had been killed in battle. She hummed along to the words as it played,

Somebody's darling, somebody's pride;
Who'll tell his mother where her boy died?

The mood quickly changed when we all laughed and sang along with "Eatin' Goober Peas."

Peas, peas, peas, peas, eatin' goober peas.
Goodness, how delicious, eatin' goober peas. "

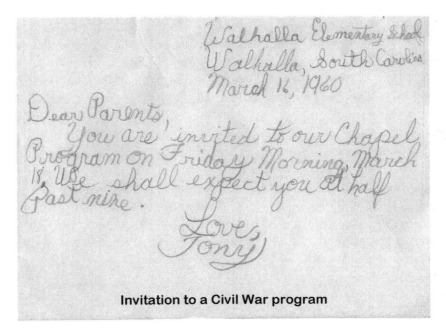

Invitation to a Civil War program

Linda was a popular name among girls born in the late 1940s and early 1950s, and there were two Lindas in Mrs. Whitmire's fifth grade class. My memories of those two Lindas remind me of a two-part song by Charles Ives, titled "Memories: A-Very Pleasant. B-Rather Sad." Obviously, the "A" part of the song describes a happy memory, and the "B" part something rather sad. As I recall these two memories, I'll refer to my classmates as Linda A. and Linda B.

After returning from lunch one February afternoon, through our classroom window we saw huge snowflakes falling, swirling, and spinning in the wind. Snowfall was a rare sight, so our eyes were glued to this wonder of Mother Nature. Even Mrs. Whitmire seemed to be fascinated. Realizing her teaching skills could not compete with this winter spectacle, Mrs. Whitmire let us go, one row at a time, to run in the snow while the rest of the class looked on.

The sheer joy of snow hitting our faces as we ran through the white powder was like magic. I watched as Linda A. closed her eyes tight, opened her mouth wide, and ran as hard as she could all the way across the schoolyard. After returning to class I suppose Linda A. had second thoughts about how she looked while running outside with her eyes shut tight and mouth wide open. No one asked, but she explained, "I was trying to eat snow."

I'll bet if Linda A. had it to do over again, she'd just run. Eyes open. Mouth closed.

Linda B. was a large, overweight girl from a poor family. She had failed the fifth grade once and was repeating it with our class. Her clothes were tattered and dirty. I don't remember her having friends, and I can only imagine what her home life was like. Linda B. didn't have a lot going for her, and I think she knew it. But Linda B. had her fifteen minutes of fame.

Our class assignment was to construct a scrapbook and to include leaves from our indigenous trees. Although Linda's experience came from the fifth grade she had failed the year before, that experience paid off as she became our in-class expert when it came to waxing leaves.

Mrs. Whitmire gave Linda B. the floor.

"You cut a piece o' wax paper about a foot long. Lay it on a arning board. Then take your leave and lay it in the middle of the wax paper. Now take another piece o' wax paper, same size as the other'n, and lay it on top of your leave. Then arn acrost the wax paper with a warm arn. Not too hot or hit'll burn it and rurn it."

We giggled. Linda B. smiled, delighted she could make a rhyming joke.

"Just hot enough so's to melt the wax around your leave. Now with a pair o' scissors, you cut around the outside aige o' your leave."

Fascinated, we listened attentively as Linda B. explained each step in detail. No fifth grader had ever thought of such an idea, and we were impressed. Some asked questions, and Linda B. answered with confidence, proving even more her depth of knowledge in waxing leaves. She beamed. It was her moment.

For that brief spell, Linda B. was an exceptional teacher. She taught our class how to preserve a leaf in wax. Fifty-five years later, I still remember her clear, detailed instructions.

I wonder where Linda B. is today. God bless her. I hope she's had many more moments like that one. I hope she's had a good life.

World Books

M y sixth grade, under Mrs. Earle, was somewhat of a turning point.

On one of the first days of class, Mrs. Earle showed us pictures of famous sights of Europe as a way of describing the places we would study about. She said, "You may think to yourself, 'Oh, I'll never go there,' but you will."

She said, "but you will" with such confidence that I believed her—and less than five years later, her words proved true: At age 17, I was standing in Westminster Cathedral in London, England. For three weeks I was immersed in European culture as Mama, Daddy, Wayne, and I toured nine countries.

That one comment by Mrs. Earle opened my mind to think in ways I had never thought before. The term "think outside the box" was not common then, but Mrs. Earle challenged us to do just that, to think beyond our current surroundings. In that regard, she was great.

Mrs. Earle's husband was our mail carrier, so when he delivered our mail, he must have spotted the two pear trees in our side yard. Obviously he told Mrs. Earle, because she asked me to bring her some pears. It felt special just to be recognized, so I picked a paper sack full and took them to her. I didn't expect to be paid; I was simply glad to do it for her. After class she gave me a half dollar and a quarter. Seventy-five cents! I thought I was rich.

Everything about the sixth grade was good. I can't exactly explain it, but I remember only feelings of optimism. The joy of learning. The joy of living. What a difference a teacher can make.

One week each year was called Parents' Week, when parents would come to school, get to know the teacher, attend class, eat lunch with their kids, etc. I can still see Mama in a nice dress and heels, walking erect with her own sense of pride and self-respect, as she carried her tray in the cafeteria. Due to her strict beliefs, Mama never cut her hair or wore makeup or jewelry, but she was attractive and refined that day. To me, she was every bit on a par with the other mothers from better homes, and it made me feel proud that she was there.

There was one minor setback that year. Oddly enough, it didn't happen in school, but it had a negative impact on my desire to learn.

A World Book Encyclopedia salesman was making the rounds. When he called on us, Mama and Daddy seemed interested at first, but decided not to buy the set. That really disappointed me. I was motivated. I was in a good, positive mental state. Wayne, Jo, Nant, and I were all still in school, and I was about to enter junior high, but the expense of purchasing a set of encyclopedias was deemed too much for Mama and Daddy's modest income.

Our church expected its members to tithe a full ten percent of their gross household income, plus give in the offering every time the collection plate was passed, plus help support a missionary, plus contribute to other church-related causes. I've heard preachers say, "You can't out-give the Lord." Well, I reckon not, since the Lord has way yonder more resources than mortal humans have. I didn't know we were in competition with the Lord anyway. And preachers love to quote the verse, "Give, and it shall be given unto you; good measure, pressed down, and shaken together, and running over..." The reward of running over with money from giving was all the encouragement some people needed to dig deeper. To give their "widow's mite." After giving so much to the church and its causes, there was barely enough left to feed, clothe, and shelter a family of six, with little for extras. Frankly, I now think some of the money we contributed to the church should have been spent on encyclopedias. But what do I know? For whatever reason, Mama and Daddy could not justify the expense of encyclopedias for our home.

Years later, I sold encyclopedias to make extra money while attending college. I still have a set of 1974 World Books that I earned as a result of my sales. With so much online information now at our fingertips, hard copy encyclopedias are essentially obsolete, but to me they represent more than facts and data. That set of encyclopedias will always have a permanent place in my home.

Encyclopedias may or may not have made a difference in my attitude toward learning, but something did. After the sixth grade, I didn't have that same zest for knowledge. The wonderful world and all the things in it didn't look so bright again for quite a while.

A song in the air

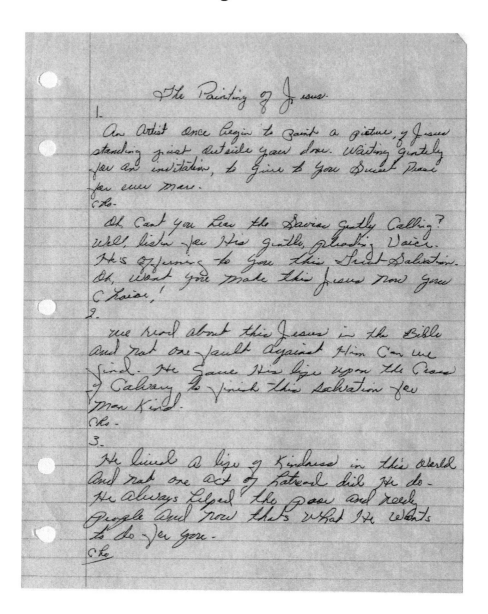

The Painting of Jesus.

1.
An Artist once began to paint a picture, of Jesus standing just outside your door. Waiting gently for an invitation, to Give to You Sweet Peace for ever more.

Cho.

Oh Cant you hear the Savior gently Calling? Well, listen for His gentle, pleading Voice. He's offering to You this Sweet Salvation. Oh, Wont you make this Jesus now your Choice!

2.
We read about this Jesus in the Bible and not one fault against Him Can we find. He gave His life upon the Cross of Calvary to finish this Salvation for Man Kind.

Cho.

3.
He lived a life of Kindness in this World and not one act of hatred did He do. He always helped the poor and needy people and now that's What He Wants to do for you.

Cho

4.

The Artist now has finished with his picture and Jesus still is standing just outside. Oh, Can't you hear Him as He's gently knocking and want you swing your hearts door open Wide?
etc

Composed:

Mrs. A.I. Deaton
Monday, July 25, 1949 – 9:30 O'clock A.M.

**Mama's song in her own hand,
signed and dated**

M ama was a gifted poet and song writer. Much of her work was tucked away and is lost, but I well remember Mama singing the song she composed, "The Painting of Jesus."

An artist once began to paint a picture
Of Jesus standing just outside your door;
Waiting gently for an invitation
To give to you sweet peace forevermore.
Oh can't you hear Him as He's gently knocking?
Just listen for His tender pleading voice;
He's offering to you a great salvation,
Oh won't you make this Jesus now your choice?

In her song, as the artist continues to paint, the second and third verses speak of Jesus' kindness and good works while on earth. And in the fourth verse, now that the painting is complete, listeners are asked how they will respond to Jesus' knocking:

The artist is now finished with his picture,
And Jesus is still standing just outside;
Waiting gently for the invitation,
Oh won't you swing your heart's door open wide?

When Mama died in 2006, a family friend, Robbie Eades, memorized Mama's song on short notice and sang it at her funeral. Needless to say, there was not a dry eye on the family pew.

W ith all his qualities, both good and bad, one cherished gift Daddy gave his children was an appreciation of music. He constantly sang around the house, while working, while driving, and whatever he was doing. Until his final days on this earth there was a song in his heart and on his lips.

While stationed overseas during World War II, Daddy made records of his singing while accompanying himself on the guitar. Against a backdrop of violence came a sweet voice from a seemingly pure heart. But like Mama's songs and poems, Daddy's records are lost, and I have no idea where they are.

How could we have been so careless with those things that were such treasures?

To quote the late Maya Angelou, "I've learned that regardless of your relationship with your parents, you'll miss them when they're gone from your life." I've learned that as well. And I'd give almost anything to have all of Mama's songs and poems, and to hear Daddy's voice on those wartime records once again.

Although he never had formal musical training, Daddy loved all types of music from country to classical. Incredibly, his favorite Christmas carol was Michael Praetorius' "Lo, How a Rose E'er Blooming." And speaking of incredible—and of different types of music—we frequently played a 78-RPM vinyl record at home titled "The Man That Comes Around," sung by Tommy Tucker. I can only assume Mama and Daddy knew that as kids, we had no idea what the song was about. And we didn't. We just thought it was funny. But it is clearly not an innocent children's song.

The verses tell of a different man who comes around each day…and for a fair price shares some intimate moments with Mama. ("Oh, Papa does the work, and Mama gets the pay…") Among the men who come around in the song are the ice man, the brush salesman, the milk man, the telephone man, and even the trash man. Anyone old enough to grow underarm peach fuzz knows that's an R-rated song in a G-rated cloak, but as kids, we didn't have a clue. Still, it's hard for me to believe our "Saint Mama" permitted that record in the house, much less allowed it to be played.

Every member of my family could sing, and sing well. Mama and Daddy sang duets in church, with Daddy taking the lead and Mama harmonizing on alto. I can still hear them singing songs of God's abiding faithfulness with comforting words such as: "I'm never alone…my Savior is with me wherever I roam." (*I'm Never Alone*), and "…you loved me when the path was so dim." (*I'd Like to Talk It All Over With Him*)

Mama (center) with my aunts Vi and Florence

And when they sang about a heavenly vacation that would last forever, the burden of everyday life was not quite as heavy:

"When I Take My Vacation in Heaven"
But when I take my vacation in Heaven
What a wonderful time that will be.
Hearing concerts by the Heavenly chorus
And the face of my Savior I'll see.
Sitting down on the banks of the river
'Neath the shade of the evergreen tree;
There I'll rest from my burdens forever.
Won't you take your vacation with me.

On a recent Father's Day, I posted a picture of Daddy on Facebook and mentioned that although he was a troubled man and made it difficult for us to love him, we did anyway. I never mentioned his singing, but everyone who knew Daddy commented about a song he and Mama sang about a weary traveler in search of that other world with all its rewards upon his arrival:

"Palms of Victory"
I saw the wayward traveler, in tattered garments clad,
And struggling up the mountain, it seemed that he was sad;
His back was laden heavy, his strength was almost gone,
But he shouted as he journeyed, "Deliverance will come!"
Then palms of victory, crowns of glory,
Palms of victory, I shall wear.

I researched that great old song and sang through every word. With each note I could hear Mama and Daddy singing along with me all the way to the final verse:

While gazing on the city, just o'er the narrow flood,
A band of holy angels came from the throne of God;
They bore him on their pinions safe o'er the dashing foam,
And joined him in his triumph, "Deliverance has come!"
Then palms of victory, crowns of glory,
Palms of victory, I shall wear.

Daddy died in 2004, Mama in 2006. I believe their deliverance has come.

On occasion, all six of us also sang in church, but none of us enjoyed it as much as Daddy. He featured himself as soloist on each verse, and the rest of the family joined in on the chorus. Nant complained about how we lined up in what she called two files (vertical rows by height). The left file was Nant in front, Jo directly behind her, and Mama at the back. The right file was me in front, then Wayne, and Daddy at the back. Nant thought it looked dumb. I guess it did.

Wayne sang bass in a gospel quartet—The Gospelaires—with our Aunt Millie, Uncle Melvin, and Melvin's brother, Larry. Wayne, Jo, Nant, and I sang in our church youth choir. We even made a long-play album with the Gospelaires Quartet on Side A and The Walhalla Number Two Church of God Youth Choir on Side B. (I'm sure some are still available if anyone's interested.)

WSNW, the Seneca radio station, gave our church the use of their studio with piano, and thirty minutes of free broadcast time each Sunday morning. The youth choir, as well as others from our church who sang solos, duets, and trios, were at the radio station every week, sending our voices over the airwaves while singing praises to the Lord.

The Deaton Trio
with Angela Long at the piano

Jo, Nant, and I sang together as The Deaton Trio and competed in the Church of God State Teen Talent contest. With me singing the lead, Jo on alto, and Nant as tenor, we won first place in the vocal ensemble category with our moving rendition of "There'll Be No Disappointments in Heaven." (Nant still has our first place plaque.)

At age nineteen, the last year I was eligible, I competed in the vocal solo category of the State Teen Talent. I placed second to a girl who couldn't sing half as well as me, but cried with every note she sang.

I should have known better. Always play for sympathy.

Jo and Nant studied piano with Mrs. Angela Long, a fine teacher and a woman we grew to love. Later, Wayne and I also took lessons from Mrs. Long, but we lacked the basic piano skills and the commitment of dedication Jo and Nant had. Both of them continued lessons for several years, became fine pianists and musicians, and still share their musical gifts.

Mrs. Long charged one dollar for a thirty-minute lesson. Two dollars an hour was good money in the 1960s, and Mama and Daddy willingly paid for our lessons. As part of our continuing music education, they also bought an eight volume, hard bound collection of piano etudes and sonatas by Mozart, Beethoven, Schumann, and

Brahms. Wayne and I weren't ready for the classics, so we played in the easy books—those with a number for each note that corresponds to a finger on the hand. It was similar to paint by numbers, except it was play by numbers. We did OK as long as our songs were in the key of C, with the thumb of our right hand playing a number 1, and the pinky a number 5. Neither Wayne nor I ever advanced to the hard bound collection of etudes and sonatas.

Wayne had big fingers, but he played from the red and white John Thompson book, "Teaching Little Fingers to Play." Nant crossed out the word "Little" and penciled in "Big." Wayne didn't care what the title said; he wanted to learn to play. He loved those hotshot gospel quartet pianists who could make the keyboard sizzle. For inspiration, Wayne played a gospel quartet record in the background while he was at the piano trying to teach his big fingers to play John Thompson. I thought his practice routine was a little strange, but I kept quiet. He never mentioned it, but Wayne may have realized that even with faithful practice, he would never match the level of play of his inspirational keyboard idols. As a result, he changed his musical focus to voice, and dedicated himself to singing gospel quartet bass.

I couldn't teach my fingers to play either. At least not very well, and not for very long. Once in frustration I expressed to Mama that I knew the notes to play, I just couldn't make my fingers play them. Mama suggested I ask Jo or Nant for advice. I didn't ask, but I suspect they would have simply said, "Practice." In the seventh grade, I did manage to perform an arrangement of "The Caissons Go Rolling Along" on a recital by Mrs. Long's students, but that was the highlight of my concertizing at the piano.

As a music major at Lee College (now Lee University), an excuse such as, "I know the notes, but I just can't get my fingers to play them" didn't go over well. A stern, "Practice!" was ordered. Only by the grace of God did I pass the required piano proficiency course. Otherwise, I might still be trying to complete my music degree.

As the saying goes, "What goes around comes around." I now teach voice at Lee University. How many times have I said to my students, "Practice!"

Funny how that works. Sometimes practice is all it takes.

We also took voice lessons from a kind and knowledgeable woman, Mrs. Acker, who lived down the street from Mrs. Long. It was Wayne's dream that the four of us would sing as a quartet with Nant on soprano, Jo as alto, me singing tenor, and Wayne on bass. Wayne's dream didn't come to fruition exactly as he hoped. We sang a few times in church, but we never had a bus with our name painted on the side, and we never made it to The Lawrence Welk Show. A few years ago, however, we began retreating to the Smoky Mountains each spring with our significant others, and along with laughing and reminiscing, a good portion of our time is spent singing in quartet style. And when we get together during the Christmas holidays, we sing Daddy's favorite carol, "Lo, How a Rose E'er Blooming," in four part harmony with Nant on soprano, Jo as alto, me singing tenor, and Wayne on bass.

Ready to sing "Lo How a Rose E'er Blooming"

It is obvious my parents placed a high value on music. We didn't have World Book Encyclopedias in our home, but we had volumes of music. Music was essential to our family, and in retrospect, I can't argue with Mama and Daddy's decision or logic. Music is one of God's greatest gifts, and our parents offered it to us through their personal love of it and by providing their children proper musical training.

And that's something for which I will always be grateful.

Hallelujah!

From as far back as I remember, I was continually surrounded by music. As a child and adolescent at home, at church, and on the local radio I was fed a steady diet of country and gospel music. Although my tastes have broadened since that time, some of the old gospel hymns are especially endearing to me still today. My good friend, soprano Jacque Culpepper, grew up singing these same hymns and said it so well, "Those old songs minister to us." And they do.

During my boyhood piano and voice lessons, and while attending senior high chorus concerts where my three siblings sang, I was slowly introduced to a different style of music—classical music. I was beginning to like it, but I had no idea what I was in store for when it was announced that the Lee College Touring Choir would give a concert at the Walhalla Number One Church of God. The church out town.

When my family arrived on the night of the concert, a Trailways bus with a broad "Lee College Touring Choir" banner was parked directly in front of the church. I knew this was big. The sanctuary was packed with members of Churches of God in the area as well as local townspeople who came to hear the choir that Saturday night in the spring of 1961. Then the sopranos, altos, tenors, and basses took their places on the risers in orderly fashion, and opened with a stirring rendition of "Glorious is Thy Name" from Mozart's *Twelfth Mass:*

Glorious is Thy name almighty Lord.
Let all heaven and earth adore.
We praise Thee.
We give thanks to Thee.
We adore Thee .
We glorify Thee.

And glorious it was! I had never in my life heard music so beautiful and powerfully moving. Professor A. T. Humphries, the conductor, left no detail unattended and gave significance to every aspect of their presence. He explained that although the choir's attire of long crimson robes draped with white shawls might be perceived as formal, it was instead a testament to God's saving grace. The crimson color symbolized the cleansing blood of Jesus and the white shawls, the confirmation of a pure heart.

This choir of select voices sang a two-hour concert of choral masterworks, hymn arrangements, and spirituals, all to the glory of God, with musical excellence and integrity. A well-known, rousing chorus to appeal to the emotions of the congregation would have been a popular end to such an evening, but Professor Humphries was wise in his ability to validate the worship value of time-honored traditional music.

Professor Humphries knew that as Pentecostals, Church of God people enjoyed a vigorous style of worship where "hallelujah" was a term frequently uttered, and sometimes shouted, as a spontaneous expression of joy and praise to God. He noted that this same expression, "hallelujah," with the same intent of joy and praise, was voiced 167 times in the great chorus they were about to perform as the choir's finale. He then told the compelling story of how the composer's assistant, after calling to him several times with no response, found the composer in his room in tears. When the assistant asked what was wrong, George Frederick Handel held up his musical manuscript to "The Hallelujah Chorus" and said, "I think I have seen the face of God."

Farmers, factory workers, good, simple men and women of faith, some with little formal education and most with no musical training or prior exposure to classical music, openly worshiped their God with hearts of adoration as the choir sang:

Hallelujah!
For the Lord God omnipotent reigneth.
The kingdom of this world is become
The kingdom of our Lord, and of His Christ,
And He shall reign forever and ever.
King of kings, and Lord of lords.
Hallelujah!

It was the proper ending to a musical celebration of God's glory, majesty, and might.

Because of that singular experience I determined in my young mind, and in my own way, that music was my calling. I wanted to attend Lee College and major in music. My dream eventually came true, and as a result, I have been given numerous opportunities not only to hear, but also to perform Handel's *Messiah* and many other grand works of various musical genres.

Since I was that sixth grader in 1961, my appreciation for and knowledge of music has grown exponentially. I have been inspired and uplifted again and again by the magic and miracle of this invaluable gift.

Music has been a constant friend through good times and bad. Schober's poetry in Schubert's art song, "An die Musik," a song I have assigned many of my voice students, expresses the gift of music and its abiding friendship:

> *You, sacred art, in many dark hours,*
> *When life's mad tumult wraps around me,*
> *You have kindled my heart to warm love,*
> *You have transported me into a better world.*

As an expression of my thanks, I have only one word. Hallelujah!

Robert's Mother

B ecause of my good marks in the sixth grade, I was placed into a high-achieving section of the seventh grade. But things didn't turn out so well. I had good teachers, but I simply lost much of my motivation and direction. In seventh grade we changed teachers every class period, and I missed the constant positive influence Mrs. Earle had provided the year before.

There certainly were bright moments, however. Mr. Seigler, who taught South Carolina history, took it upon himself to "socialize" us with parties—complete with dress-up attire, sandwiches, and dancing.

In seventh grade

Yes, dancing (even though I conveniently failed to tell Mama and Daddy such worldliness was taking place).

Mrs. Ballenger, who ran a dance studio in town, came to one of our parties and offered free dance instruction. That's when I dared to stick my toe into the ocean of social wickedness. At arm's length, I danced with Eleanor Ninestein, who was one of the most popular girls in school, and was also the smartest person in our class. Even though Mama and Daddy weren't privy to the information, I later bragged to my buddy Ken Harmon that I had danced with Eleanor at the party. He was impressed. So was I.

Mr. Seigler also took our South Carolina History class to the Cyclorama in Atlanta to see a depiction of the Civil War. We left the school grounds in a chartered bus early on a Saturday morning, and had barely gotten beyond the city limits when Dallon Weathers belted out (to the tune of "Oh, When the Saints Go Marching In"):

Oh, when the South shall rise again.
Oh, when the South shall rise again.
Oh Lord, I'd hate to be a Yankee,
When the South shall rise again.

That familiar refrain surfaced off and on throughout the trip.

Mama had packed an entire box of Cheez-Its as my snack. They were good! I still love them to this day. But how's this for dietetic mockery: I was recently diagnosed with celiac disease, and I can no longer abide Cheez-Its or any other food product containing gluten. Nevertheless, they always remind me of Mama and that bus trip to the Cyclorama.

At about 11:30 we stopped for lunch at a roadside diner. Once we were seated, I was awestruck when Peggy Brown strolled over to the jukebox, popped in a dime, pushed the buttons, and out boomed "Big Bad John." I'd never played a song on a jukebox in my life—and never had an extra dime to spend on one. But Peggy was cool. She knew her way around a café jukebox. Amazing.

It's funny how things can happen, but the significance of the moment doesn't occur until many years later. Although I was timid and insecure, I wasn't aware that the other kids didn't necessarily associate with me. I did have a few classmates that I thought of as friends, and if I was being snubbed I was oblivious to it. On the bus to Atlanta I sat by myself, quiet and rather content while others around me were much more gregarious.

Mrs. Phillips, my friend Robert Phillips' mother, had gone along on the trip as one of the chaperones. She sat with another chaperone, Billy Darby's mother, at the front of the bus next to Mr. Seigler, talking, laughing, and smoking. (Can you believe smoking in public was a common practice in those days?) At one point, I noticed Mrs. Phillips looking toward the rear of the bus at the students. She called her son Robert to the front and spoke to him briefly. As he returned to the back of the bus, Robert sat down beside me and started a conversation.

At the time, I was completely unaware of Mrs. Phillips' kind gesture. But over the years, that scene has replayed in my mind, and I realize what a thoughtful thing she did. I will never forget her act of charity to a shy kid like me.

I already had somewhat of an interest in Civil War history, and our trip to the Cyclorama left a lasting impression. The pictures in my history book were no comparison to the panoramic portrayal of war in harsh realism. Within only a few feet of me lay the twisted wreckage of a demolished railroad track, the destruction of homes and buildings, and the carnage of Union and Rebel soldiers. Devastation was everywhere. But the most gripping depiction of all was the true account of one soldier dressed in blue, giving a drink of water to another wounded soldier dressed in grey. The sad irony of the scene, as explained by our guide, was that those soldiers on opposite sides of war were brothers. Brother against brother.

Showtime

I was placed into a different section in the eighth grade, but I didn't mind. There were good teachers and good students, a lot of whom were my friends from seventh grade, who also had been reassigned. Miss McDaniel (we called her "Ma Daniel," but certainly not to her face) was my homeroom teacher. She decided her homeroom class should perform a Halloween play, and I was cast as one of the leads.

This was possibly one of the best things to happen to me, because as a result I began to break out of my shell.

On stage, I didn't have to be that shy, unsure kid. I could be anything I wanted. During the play, I consciously made an exaggerated stage gesture, as if frightened, and it got a huge laugh. That one bit of impromptu staging paid dividends in popularity. As I walked to the bus that afternoon, my friend Brantley Gasque told me I should be a movie star. Eighth-grade folly or otherwise, that was superb reassurance.

No Friday night lights

J unior high school was OK, but I felt cheated out of many good memories. Those unreasonable church teachings kept me from doing almost everything except participating in musical activities.

The thing I wanted most to do was attend football games with other students every Friday night. Oh, hell no! That was considered "worldly amusement." I was so ashamed of this predicament that I contrived a way to get around it. I was pretty good at picking up game information from the other students' conversations, and I later parroted what I'd heard so I could pretend I'd been there. I wanted so much to be a part of the excitement of the game, the crowd, the cheers, the scores, the wins.

But no. What screwed-up beliefs.

A few years later our school newspaper, *The Echo*, wanted us graduating seniors to submit a humorous, ridiculous prank to be printed as our favorite high school memory. Different ones recalled funny incidents and wondered how they got away with them without being caught. "Remember the time before the Seneca game when we dressed that life-size dummy up like the Seneca quarterback and hung it from the goal post?" one student laughed. "And after the Junior-Senior prom, we took that 'ICE COLD BEER SOLD HERE' sign from the beer joint in West Union and put it on the roof of the school." All my classmates' memories were related to sports, sock-hops, or proms. Although I laughed, I felt resentful as I listened to them tell their stories, because I couldn't think of a single thing to write.

I have empathy for other kids of that era whose forced-upon religious teachings kept them from having typical teenage fun.

Makes me mad to this day.

No trespassing

C ountry life was mighty good year 'round, but summer was the best season of all. The highlight of summer was a visit to the ol' swimmin' hole.

In the country, there was no such thing as a proper pool like the one at the Walhalla Recreation Center, where the water was so clear you could see a dime on the bottom of the deep end. That's where the city kids went. For us country folks, our cool relief from the hot sun was the chilly waters of a local creek. Our favorite swimmin' hole was a place we had gone for years: Oconee Creek. It was ideal in size and depth, with a big tree root near the water line which served as a natural diving board.

After supper on weeknights, Wayne, Jo, Nant, and I were sure to get the chores finished early, and then it would start.

"Daddy, can we go swimming?"

First response: "Naaaaw, I don't thank so." Daddy could always stretch his answers loooong.

"Daddy, can we go swimming?"

Second response: "I'm kinda tired."

"Daddy, can we go swimming?"

Third response: "It's gettin' late.

"Daddy, can we go swimming?"

Then came Daddy's questions. "Milk the cow?"

"Yep."

"Take up the eggs?"

"Yep."

"Housework done?"

"Yep."

(The whole time we're thinking, we could be there by now!)

"Well, go ask your Mama."

Hot dog! We knew Mama would say yes.

At the swimmin' hole, Wayne and I spent most of our time swimming, belly-busting, and cannon-balling into the 4½-foot "deep" end while Mama, who was scared to death of water, stayed safely on the bank and constantly cautioned, "You boys be careful!"

Jo and Nant waded in the shallow end, the hems of their school dresses floating on the water's surface, because they didn't dare wear something as immodest as bathing suits.

Swimming with a person of the opposite sex ("mixed bathing") was against the teachings of the church—and to Daddy, this also applied to members of your immediate family. We had heard the shameful tales of families from our local church who swam together, clad only in skimpy bathing suits. But Daddy, a loyal member of the Walhalla Number Two Church of God (again), believed in following its teachings to the letter. There was no compromise when it came to "mixed bathing." Except for shoes, we were fully dressed. Yes, that meant Wayne and I even wore T-shirts and overall britches.

Then came that eventful Tuesday evening in June. We proceeded, as usual, to what had been our "Oconee Creek Swimmin' Hole" but what had suddenly become the "T.S. Hunnicutt Swimmin' Hole."

The trailhead at the main road was posted with a big sign: "NO TRESPASSING."

Anybody who's ever lived in the country knows the local swimming hole belongs to every person in the community. The fact it might be on someone's private property is never considered. But the "NO TRESPASSING" sign made it clear that T. S. now owned the swimming hole, and outsiders were not allowed to swim in it.

As unfriendly, un-neighborly, un-community-minded, and downright un-Christian as this was, everybody accepted T. S.'s decision.

Everybody, that is, except Daddy.

Nobody, especially T.S. Hunnicutt, was going to tell Daddy where he and his family could or could not swim.

T.S. and Daddy had what you might call "a history." Although they were kin, or perhaps because they were kin, there had been bad blood between them for years. I think Daddy hated him.

We were having a fun time swimming, diving, and wading when T.S. showed up and in a measured, steely voice said to Daddy, "Didn't you see 'at posted sign?"

Mama, sensing the tension of the moment, hurried Wayne, Jo, Nant, and me out of the creek and was preparing to leave as soon as possible.

But Daddy was not about to leave. Not yet, anyway.

I was drying the creek water out of my ears, so I didn't hear exactly what was said. But I suspect Daddy said something like, "You can take 'at posted sign and shove it..." Whatever Daddy said, T.S. was not amused.

To the contrary, he became quite contrary.

By now, Mama had scurried Jo and Nant up the trail and back to our car, but Wayne and I stayed to see what was about to happen. A "rite of passage" of sorts, I suppose. So, this is how grown men settle their disputes?

One heated word led to another. Then came the ultimatum. Daddy demanded: "Well, what'cha gonna do about it, T. S.?"

Up to this point, it had been all words. The kind of words Wayne and I, and every other boy, had heard on the schoolyard when a fight was brewing. But these were not boys. These were grown men.

T. S. had reached the tipping point.

"I'll show you what I'm gonna do about it!" He balled up his fists and began to circle.

I was somewhere between amused and confused. But Wayne, more aware of the gravity of the situation, was growing more nervous by the second. To relieve his anxiety during this disgusting diatribe, Wayne unconsciously took out his pocket knife and began cleaning his fingernails.

"Awright, just calm down," Wayne suddenly spat. "You both got too hot and you just need to calm down." Wayne showed more poise and maturity than these two childish adults who were about to come to blows.

T. S. unfolded his fists and said to Daddy: "He's got a knife, so we better do what he says."

Disgusted, Wayne asked in the most sarcastic tone, "Did you *really* think I was gonna cut you?"

Nevertheless, for the moment anyway, the tension eased. Daddy finally said something sensible: "Come on boys, let's go."

As we made our way along the dirt path, T. S. trailed us like a hound dog to make sure we were leaving.

Now, talk about timing! I wouldn't have believed this if I hadn't seen it myself, but just as we climbed the bank to the road, a deputy sheriff's car came cruising by. T. S., obviously convinced beyond a reasonable doubt that his actions were well within the law, flagged it down.

When that deputy got out of his squad car, Lord, did he look big! He must have been six foot, four inches tall, and he must have weighed at least two hundred and fifty pounds. The name on his stiff creased shirt read, "Hurt." That alone struck me as both scary and comical.

Deputy Hurt had barely stretched his tall frame to full form before T. S. began badgering him. "This family ain't nothin' but trusspaissers, and when I tried to throw 'em offa my land, that boy here pulled a knife on me!"

"Pfft! C'mon, T.S.! You know I wudden gonna cut you!" Wayne said.

Mama, Jo, and Nant had been safely perched in our car, with their fingers in their ears, so if later questioned about the encounter, they could say in all honesty they hadn't heard a thing. But when Deputy Hurt arrived, Mama bolted from the car to stand by her man. The law was involved now. She knew Daddy was not altogether in the right, but she wasn't going to let him be thrown in jail without a fight.

Deputy Hurt was aware of the ways of country folks, so he more or less blew the whole thing off. "Why can't y'all git along?" he said, in disgust. "Now stop this fussin' and fightin' and act like somebody!" With that, he folded his big frame back into the squad car, slammed the door, and drove away.

T. S. was incensed at Deputy Hurt's dismissive attitude and was in no mood to get along with or act like anybody but his mean self. "This thang ain't over, you know!" he warned Daddy. "But I ain't gonna fight you right here in front o' your wife 'n kids."

"I'll fight you anywhere, anytime!" Daddy challenged. "You jes' name the time and the place!"

T. S. met Daddy's dare with, "Aw right. Meet me right here tomorrow night at six o'clock, and we'll settle this thang once and for all, by God!"

Before Daddy could finalize the deal, Mama leaned toward him and whispered under her breath, "Tomorrow's Wednesday. You can't fight on Wednesday night. You gotta go to prayer meetin'."

T.S. grabbed the door handle of his '56 Crown Victoria. He plopped into the seat like an anvil, cranked and revved the V-8 engine, then yelled, "Stay offa my land!" His Ford lunged ahead like a rocket. As we stood in the wake of its angry spinning tires, the grass and gravel swirled around us.

Finally the dust settled, and the excitement was over. For a moment, Mama, Daddy, Wayne, Jo, Nant, and I stood motionless. Then we pulled ourselves forward and found our places in the Bel Air. After all the hostile drama, the familiar beige and brown interior of the ol' Chevy seemed to say, "Welcome home, weary traveler." But an awkward silence hung in the air as thick as sorghum molasses.

Without a word, Daddy stared straight ahead, his face as pale as a corpse. He inserted the key into the ignition, turned the switch, depressed the clutch, pulled the gearshift into low, released the clutch, and steered the car into motion.

As the "NO TRESSPASSING" sign faded in the rear view mirror, Daddy shifted into second gear, and Mama whispered, "You s'pose to lead singin' too."

Dexter, Russell, Reid, and Me

Dexter LeCroy, Russell Addis, and Reid Morgan were my best childhood friends. The four of us went to church together and were in the same Sunday school class. I was the oldest, with Dexter one year behind, and Russell and Reid a year younger than Dexter. Until we were old enough to drive and have our own cars, every Sunday we begged our parents to let us go to each other's house and play ball. We played till suppertime, and then it was Sunday night church at 7:30.

Once Dexter and I were at a revival service when a smoking sinner flung a used pack of Winstons through the church window as he laid aside the weight of sinful tobacco that had so easily beset him. After church, under the cover of darkness, we retrieved the Winstons—only three left in the pack— and decided to give nicotine a try. We met in the graveyard the next night before church, hunkered down behind a tall tombstone, and lit up. Ah… only twelve years old and smoking a filtered Winston.

My cousin Larry had told me if you chew pine needles it will take the smell of cigarettes off your breath, so Dexter and I stripped a handful from a low-hanging limb, stuffed them in our mouths, and chewed fast. Oh, that bitter taste. The pine needles worked and we didn't get caught, but we were out of Winstons. As the revival continued and one sinner after another repented, Dexter and I waited for another dramatic deliverance from tobacco, but it never happened.

Our pleasures of sin were but for a season.

Russell always had a big grin on his face. He lived farther away than Dexter and Reid so I didn't see him as often, but when I did, it was fun. I could count on Russell for some harmless mischief. Well, maybe not so harmless.

We nearly got stampeded by an ornery ol' bull in the pasture behind Russell's house. Russell, his younger brother Steve, and I dared to climb the fence and step inside, but the bull was in no mood for visitors. He turned and charged in our direction, and I swear there was smoke coming out of his flared nostrils. Russell and I jumped the fence, and Steve raced through a thick patch of pines. We waited outside, and after a while the bull calmed down and ambled out of sight. When the coast was clear, we called for Steve to come back, but he had run so far into the woods he got lost. When Russell and I found him, he was still shaking.

Although Reid was my closest neighbor, he went to the Keowee County School, and I attended the school in Walhalla. I didn't know him very well until he showed up at my house with a football tucked under his arm and said, "Wanna play ball?" We became best buddies and lifelong friends.

Reid loved country living as much as I did, and the acres of trees, creeks, hills, and hollers around our homes were ideally suited for us to tramp and roam among the tadpoles, turtles, lizards, rabbits, and squirrels. Lucky for us, snakes were scarce, and we rarely saw one. Barns and outbuildings were ideal for hideouts and a secret "No girls allowed" club house.

I pity any boy with barely a hint of the spirit of adventure who never knew the joys of growing up in the country. That's the part of my childhood I wouldn't trade with anybody.

There is nothing like camping out with your buddies. One summer night the four of us—Dexter, Russell, Reid, and I—camped in the feed room of the barn at my house. The hay bales were great for sleeping, but sleep was the last thing on our minds. We had talked and talked for hours when suddenly the kitchen light come on up at my house. At first I was confused, but I soon realized Mama was already up fixing breakfast. I couldn't believe we had talked all night long.

Reid and I camped out a lot, and most of the time we just slept under the stars. Neither of us had a tent or even a sleeping bag, but in the summer, a quilt below us and a blanket over us was enough. We never got cold, because everybody knows when you camp out, you sleep in your clothes. (Although there was one time when my Sunday school class camped on the banks of Burnt Tanyard River, and a city boy changed into his PJs before crawling into his store-bought sleeping bag. Poor boy. He didn't know any better. Life was a little rough for him for a while after that.)

In the pasture beyond my house, Reid and I laid down our camping gear on a grassy, level spot near a huge weeping willow tree. We threw our hunting knives and hatchets at the tree until we thought we were experts. With our deadly weapons, we were fearless of any intruders, human or otherwise, so we decided to bed down. We were sleeping well until about one in the morning, when we were startled by an unfamiliar sound. "What's that?" I whispered.

With the courage of Davy Crockett, Reid grabbed his hunting knife and said, "I don't know, but I'm gonna find out."

As it turned out, we didn't need to follow the sound, because the sound was in search of us. One of Granny Deaton's cats must have smelled our sandwiches and was looking for a midnight snack. Of course we didn't do her any harm; we just made it clear to the kitty she was not welcome and shooed her away.

Real men of the wild, we were.

Reid and I also camped out in cold winter months with layers of coats, pants, and socks, and a campfire to keep warm. One night, as it got colder, we added more wood, stoked the fire, and edged closer. I was sitting on the ground Indian-style with my feet only inches from the fire when all of a sudden, from out of the sole of my shoe a flame shot forth like a welder's torch. My shoe was on fire! I jumped up and dug my foot in the dirt to put it out, while Reid busted out laughing. We stayed the whole night with no tent, no sleeping bag – just two crazy country boys and a campfire. The next morning, we cooked eggs over a can of sterno and drank coffee from our thermos jugs.

When I saw Reid at church the following Sunday, he said his mother told him the night we camped out the temperature had plunged to seventeen degrees.

"Ha ha!" I laughed. "But my feet never got cold."

Dexter eventually became co-owner of a successful construction company in South Carolina. We'd pretty much lost touch with each other until he brought his daughter to enroll for classes at Lee

University where I was teaching. Being out of touch for years didn't matter. Still good friends.

At our home church's one hundredth anniversary in 2014, a bald-headed stranger came running up to me with an outstretched hand, grinning from ear to ear. I should have recognized his devilish eyes, but I just grinned back, shook his hand, and asked, "Who are you?"

"Russell Addis," he said. Then I knew. Yep, it was ol' Russell. He'd become a preacher. Who woulda thought it? Not me.

Reid and I attended Lee College together and both studied music. He met and later married a lovely and incredibly talented pianist, Sharon Abbott. For a number of years, Reid and Sharon worked as music ministers in Michigan, Florida, Georgia, and South Carolina. Then in 1983, after repeated tests for unexplained vision and muscle control issues, Sharon received sobering news. She was diagnosed with multiple sclerosis.

Suzy and me with Reid and Sharon

In her book, "My Strength and My Song," Sharon refers to Reid as her Prince Charming. I can see why. On the day Sharon learned she had M.S., she tearfully relayed the diagnosis to Reid. As the news quietly sank in, Reid took her hand and said, "Don't forget that you always have God, and you always have me. Neither of us will leave you. With His help, we're going to get through this."

Reid and Sharon moved near Roanoke, Virginia, to be closer to family. Recently, while attending the Tinker Mountain Writers Workshop at Hollins University, Suzy and I met Reid and Sharon for dinner. The restaurant staff was kind and patient as over dinner, dessert, glasses of iced tea, and mugs of coffee Reid and I relived stories from our past.

Great times. Great friends.

Sharon was right. A Prince Charming.

A perfect day

I t was Labor Day. Wayne was about to enter his senior year of high school and would graduate in May. Jo would be in the tenth grade, Nant in the ninth, and I in the seventh. We were growing up—and fast. According to the calendar, from that first Monday in September there were nearly three more weeks before the beginning of autumn, when the leaves would change color and the air would turn crisp. But in only one day, school would be in full session and the lazy, carefree days of summer would be over.

Wayne, Jo, Nant, Mama, Daddy and me about 1961

Until that year, I never remember our family acknowledging Labor Day as a holiday. There was always work to be done, and Daddy's attitude was that Labor Day should be spent as a day of labor. But for some reason this year was different. Somewhere in the galaxy the stars aligned themselves as never before, because we planned a family outing at the river. Years later, I learned what may have been the motivation for this day, but I reveled in the present without questioning its perfection.

That morning, we packed and loaded picnic supplies and drove to the Quentin Deaton Hole, a secluded place on Uncle Quentin's property that only a few people knew about. We trudged through the thick weeds and underbrush to the river's edge, totin' a pot of Mama's green beans, a chicken, potato chips, paper plates, cups, napkins, plastic spoons and forks, charcoal, lighter fluid, matches, folding chairs, blankets, a gallon of sweet tea, towels, an extra set of clothes for swimming, two inner tubes, an iron skillet, and a watermelon.

On the shore of the river, a wide sandy beach stretched to the water's edge with plenty of room to set up the chairs and lay the blankets. Away from the shore near the tree line, someone had made a crude but effective cooking space with a metal grate laid across a rectangular shape of standing rocks. The river's current was steady but not too strong, good for both tubing and swimming. About halfway across the river, a huge, flat platform rock lay below the water's surface and was just right for diving or playing "last man standing"—a wrestling match of sorts with no rules, where each man pushed, pulled, grabbed, tripped, or whatever to try and throw the other man off the rock and into the deep.

As soon as everything was hauled in and set up, Wayne and I hit the water and swam out to the flat rock and then back. "Come on Daddy, get in!" we shouted.

"All right boys, now I'll show you the American Legion stroke I learned in the Army." Daddy jumped in and swam to the rock with us trailing in his wake. Mama had settled into a folding chair and was taking in the warm sun. Jo and Nant (in dresses, of course) made themselves comfortable on the inner tubes and splashed Daddy, Wayne, and me in the face anytime we swam near them. We laughed and splashed them back. "Stop!" they hollered, but we kept splashing until they clutched their inner tubes and ran on shore. That scene played out over and over.

I never remember a single day so full of joy, and so free of tension. Daddy was jovial and full of fun. Mama seemed peaceful, smiling at our play. Jo and Nant were happy wading, tubing, and teasing Daddy, Wayne, and me with their splashing. Wayne and I swam and played for a good two hours. Then we stole the inner tubes from Jo and Nant and snoozed until they sneaked up and tipped us over.

After a full morning of fun, Daddy built a fire and Mama fried the chicken in the iron skillet and warmed up the green beans. Fried chicken, green beans, potato chips, sweet tea, and watermelon. Just shut up.

After we ate, Mama made us wait thirty minutes before going back in the water so we wouldn't get cramps. When it was safe, we dove in and swam and played "last man standing" till time to go home.

By late afternoon we started packing to leave. It had been such a good day we were in no hurry, but we'd had about all the fun we could stand for one day. It was a perfect day, and none of us wanted it to end. On that one day there was a rare, priceless love, harmony, and fun I'd never experienced. We were the quintessential "Father Knows Best" family.

At home that evening, we relived the fun time we'd had, recounting every stroke, splash, laugh, scream, and every mouthful of fried chicken, green beans, potato chips, sweet tea, and watermelon. The good feelings lingered until bedtime.

So, why was that day so different? Why did we celebrate *that* Labor Day with family, fun, and food? For years I never knew why; I only remembered that Labor Day as one of the fondest memories of all my childhood.

Years later, as Daddy and I talked at a family gathering, I recalled our Labor Day of '61. He didn't use the word *premonition*, but I was struck by what he said. "I had a feeling that day.....somehow I just knew that we'd never all be together like that again."

This was from a man who I thought never had tender emotions.

It was the most poignant moment I'd ever spent with Daddy. He did have feelings. He was aware that in a few short years his children would be adults. Soon we'd have to part. And when the sun set on that Labor Day of 1961, our perfect day ended.

When you come to the end of a Perfect Day,
And you sit alone with your thought;
While the chimes ring out with a carol gay,
For the joy that the day has brought.
Do you think what the end of a Perfect Day
Can mean to tired heart;
When the sun goes down with a flaming ray,
And the dear hearts have to part?
                    Carrie Jacobs-Bond

Miss Brandt

In the eighth grade I joined the junior high chorus which, in retrospect, was one of the smartest decisions I ever made. In chorus, I could share my vocal talents and be recognized for them. I also found a new mentor in Miss Henrietta Brandt, the chorus teacher who would prove to be a very positive influence in my life. Miss Brandt showered me with praises and compliments, and I began to believe in myself. Or at least in my vocal skills.

At home, it was a constant uphill struggle for identity and self-awareness. I never felt challenged or motivated to have goals, dreams, or aspirations beyond my immediate surroundings. It was all church: Jesus is coming soon! Maybe tonight! Keep your lamp trimmed and burning. You'd better watch how you live every second of every day.

All that was different with Miss Brandt. She was a devout Lutheran of German descent, and proud to profess her Christian faith, but she wasn't a nut about it.

Miss Brandt was a fine choral teacher, and she was an even better person who truly cared about her "chilluns," as she called us. All of Miss Brandt's students respected her.

She had only two simple rules:

1. Be a lady.
2. Be a gentleman.

We knew exactly what those rules meant, and Miss Brandt expected her students to abide by them.

Miss Brandt saw talent in me that I didn't know existed; with her encouragement, I began to recognize it myself. She *believed* in me. I dearly loved her, and I felt loved by her.

I continued in Miss Brandt's chorus all the way through high school. I did average work in my other classes, but I excelled in chorus. For the first time ever, *I* was the teacher's pet. In chorus, I was the equivalent of Annie Bailes *and* Eleanor Ninestein. What a switch! Miss Brandt showcased my talent at every opportunity, and publicly commended my vocal abilities when we performed.

In 2002, my wife Suzy and I were celebrating the Christmas holidays with family in Walhalla when I learned that Miss Brandt, now ninety years old, had been moved to an assisted living facility in nearby West Union. We had kept in contact over the years, and any time I was home, I tried to see her. I knew she was getting old, so I didn't want to miss this chance to see her again. When I visited, Miss Brandt appeared alert but slightly confused. Although she never called me by name, I think she knew who I was, but I was never quite sure. With great fondness, we laughed and talked about the years I was in her chorus. I told her again that she had made a huge impact on my life, and I owed much of my success to her.

As I was leaving, I asked her if we could sing the prayer we sang before every concert she conducted. Together we quietly sang:

Dear God, creator of all music,
Be with us as we sing today.
Make our hearts and minds in tune with Thee.
Give magic to our minstrelsy.
And bring some troubled soul to Thee through our singing.
Amen.

Miss Brandt with the high school chorus
I am 5th from right, top row

With Miss Brandt when I sang at the Peace Center in Greenville, SC

When we finished, Miss Brandt looked at me with childlike innocence and said, "I wrote that, didn't I?" I wasn't sure who the composer was, but I smiled and said with complete assurance, "Yes you did, and it's beautiful." I am emotional now as I think back to that moment.

There is truth, and there is the spirit of truth.

We clasped our hands together tightly as we stood in the doorway of her little apartment. Then we embraced and bid, "Auf Wiedersehen."

I was at home in Tennessee when Miss Brandt died only one month later. When I learned the day and time of the funeral, I knew I had to attend. Suzy and I left home early on Saturday morning, February 1, 2003. During the four-hour drive to South Carolina, Suzy listened patiently as I relayed my memories of Miss Brandt. Her funeral was at the church she loved, Saint John's Evangelical Lutheran on Main Street in Walhalla. The service was a beautiful tribute to a great lady: sincere, simple, and straightforward

I do not have adequate words to express my deep affection for Miss Henrietta C. Brandt, and neither can I express my appreciation for her impact on my life.

Poliakoff's

A Christmas banquet? We'd never had one of those. It was Preacher Bell's idea. He wanted to have a Christmas banquet for the youth of the church.

Preacher Bell was the new pastor at Walhalla Number Two Church of God, and his energy and enthusiasm were already making an impact on our community. I always liked him. He could preach hell fire and brimstone in the pulpit, but he also knew how to tell a joke, laugh, and have a good time. He related well with just about everybody, and the young people loved him, especially when he mentioned a Christmas banquet.

I was in my early teens when the idea surfaced. Although we were a small church, we had a large youth group, and we loved parties. Davenport Funeral Home was generous in loaning us chairs for our social events. We'd put the chairs in a circle, and the boys would sit on one side, slumped over, munching chips and drinking Cokes, while the girls tried to get us to play games. But as details of the banquet unfolded, it became apparent this would be an entirely different type of social gathering. This event would represent the high-water mark for quality entertainment, complete with a proper meal and a dress code.

The entire rear quarter of Seigler's Steak House in Walhalla was reserved for this special occasion. December 16 was the projected date, and the excitement grew with each passing day. There were conversations about the menu, the decorations, the entertainment, and of course, what to wear. I was not nearly as concerned with the menu, decorations and entertainment, but now that I was entering the golden teenage era, I was becoming more interested in appearance.

Until this young juvenile phase in my life, I didn't need anything that resembled "dress clothes." Even at those seventh-grade dance parties, I'd worn Wayne's hand-me-down suit. The only occasion for which I had to actually dress up in the slightest was Sunday school and preaching service, and a permanent-press shirt and pants were more than adequate for that. But now, as a teenager with an impending date of such importance approaching, it was time to consider a complete ensemble, including a sport coat and tie.

In Walhalla, there were four places of business to choose from when it came to fine clothing.

There was a department store called The Fair, which was in no way indicative of the quality of its merchandise; it was actually pretty nice. However, the clientele consisted primarily of mature women and mothers with children—not exactly where a guy on the threshold of early manhood wanted to be seen making purchases.

There was Collins Department Store, which carried a solid line of clothes for the entire family. But I wanted something that was unmistakably that of a teenager.

The ideal place would have been Moore's Men's Store. Moore's had nice clothes, but the prices were a little steep for our family budget. And although I never believed it, it was rumored Mr. Moore purchased irregulars at a suit factory in Loganville, Georgia, and then sold them at regular retail prices.

Finally, there was Poliakoff's. Yes, Poliakoff's. Not Wilson's, not Johnson's, not Cooper's, nor any other southern Christian name. It was Poliakoff's.

The Poliakoffs (pronounced "Polly-coughs" by the locals) were the single token Jewish family in Walhalla.

There was Mr. and Mrs. Poliakoff, a son Robert, and a daughter Dale. They owned and operated a dry goods store on Main Street which was generally considered to be the best place in town for clothes and shoes. Thus, the decision was made that Poliakoff's was the place to shop for my new wardrobe.

Mr. and Mrs. Poliakoff were reserved in their manner and speech—"in the style of the old country," as the saying goes. They were the kind of people you said "yes, sir," "no sir," "yes ma'am," and "no ma'am" to. They owned a lovely home in a nice neighborhood alongside other respected Christian citizens. Robert and Dale attended the public school, ate in the school cafeteria, drank from the same water fountains, and used the same bathrooms as the rest of the Gentile student body.

However, this surface layer of respect was quite thin, and such "equalities" were somewhat superficial. There was a constant undercurrent of resentment and suspicion toward those who refused to accept Jesus as the Messiah.

As Mama, Daddy, and I approached Poliakoff's store, we saw in the display window a teenage mannequin dressed in a smart navy blazer with shiny brass buttons, grey pants, a white shirt, and a red tie. Did that ever look sharp!

Mama, seeing my eyes glued to the display, commented, "That's real pretty, but if we buy that for you, it'll have to be your Santa Claus." I was a little disappointed but willing to accept the compromise, because this could prove to be a wise investment into my teenage future.

Mr. Poliakoff knew our family, and as we stepped inside the store, he greeted us with genuine courtesy. "Good evening, Mr. and Mrs. Deaton. Hello, son. How may I help you?"

"Evening, Mr. Polly-cough," Daddy replied in a rather dry tone. Mama smiled and nodded. Mrs. Poliakoff then approached Mama and greeted her with the same politeness. "Hello, Mrs. Deaton. Let's look over in the ladies department while these men shop."

"Well, OK," Mama agreed, and they made their way to the opposite side of the store.

"So, gentlemen, what can I interest you in?" Mr. Poliakoff asked. "A shirt? A pair of pants?"

I don't know what triggered Daddy's mind at that point. He had always been sensitive about money (along with most everything else). Maybe he interpreted Mr. Poliakoff's question as an insult. Perhaps he thought Mr. Poliakoff was implying we could afford *only* a shirt or a pair of pants, and that's why he didn't suggest we purchase a coat and tie as well. And, of course, the fact that Mr. Poliakoff was a Jew presented a constant open invitation to crack that delicate veneer of respect.

Whatever it was, something sure struck a raw nerve in Daddy, causing his "condition" to flare up. I suppose the proper term for his condition would be "acute paranoia."

A few weeks earlier, I had been kidded at school about something and it embarrassed me.

"Don't be so paranoid," teased this little smart-aleck girl with precision curls in her hair.

"What's that?" I asked.

"Oh, don't be so defensive," she instructed, as if she had the wisdom of King Solomon. "You act like you got a big chip on your shoulder."

I knew what it meant to have a chip on your shoulder, and I reasoned if that's what paranoia was, Daddy sure had it. And he had suffered with it for as long as I could remember.

Such a thorn in the flesh would have disabled a lesser man. Not Daddy. He was determined to fight back at every opportunity. He dealt with his affliction by refusing to accept its existence. However, this denial did not prevent the symptoms from manifesting themselves from time to time, often with little or no warning.

Due to his chronic insecurities, Daddy became somewhat testy with Mr. Poliakoff, and answered with, "No, we want 'at blue coat an' 'em grey pants like you got in that winder there! You got it in his size?"

There was a distinct edge to Daddy's voice, but I'm not sure if Mr. Poliakoff noticed it. He appeared oblivious to Daddy's sharp tongue and simply replied with his usual courtesy, "Oh, I think so. What's your pants length, son?"

Before I could respond, Daddy barked out, "He don't know how long his pants are! Ain't they s'pose to come down to the top o' his shoes?"

I think Mr. Poliakoff suspected something then, because he had a quizzical look on his face. He became quiet and withdrawn.

Daddy, now confident he had scored a blow for the poor and downtrodden, stood proud. He squared his shoulders and jutted his defiant chin in preparation for the next verbal assault.

Mr. Poliakoff, ever the professional, attempted to humor the situation. He calmly asked, "You plan to wear this to church on Sunday, son?"

"YES, SIR!" Daddy's voice thundered with the fervor of a street-corner evangelist. "GONNA WEAR THAT TO CHURCH ON SUNDAY! GONNA WEAR THAT TO WORSHIP JESUS CHRIST THE LORD!"

As if the cavalry had been summoned, Mama suddenly appeared. Ever the peacemaker, she tried to address the situation as best she could by changing the subject.

"Boy, that coat 'n pants sure look good! Don't you want to put a white shirt and red tie with that?"

"Awright," Daddy ordered Mama. "Git it 'n pay the man. Let's go."

Mr. Poliakoff didn't say anything. He didn't need to. The expression on his face spoke for him. There was an awkward silence as he completed the written order.

"That comes to $37.21, including tax, Mrs. Deaton."

Returning the change from the two twenties Mama gave him, Mr. Poliakoff forced a faint smile and gently said, "Thank you, Mrs. Deaton."

He never acknowledged Daddy again. But as I reached to take my new outfit, Mr. Poliakoff shook my hand and softly said, "Merry Christmas, son."

"Merry Christmas, Mr. Polly-cough."

Capital city

T he summer between my freshman and sophomore years of high school, our family took a trip to our nation's capital, Washington, D.C. It was the farthest I'd ever been away from home.

My aunt and uncle, Millie and Melvin, had traveled to D.C. the year before, and Millie was proud to show with a red pen the long distance she and Melvin had driven from Walhalla to Washington. Poor but proud, Daddy couldn't let Millie and Melvin one-up us, so D.C. became our vacation destination.

Many of the sights were free, so to save a few dollars, we took the self-guided tour of the capital. I was awestruck as we walked along the reflecting pool on the National Mall where, at one end, stood the Washington Monument, a 555-foot-tall tribute to our nation's first president. Wayne and I were tempted to chug up the 897 steps, but the line circled all the way around the outside, and a sign read an hour and a half wait. We passed up the wait and the walk, but craned our necks at the colossal white marble obelisk and wondered what the view was like from the top. "I'll bet you can see all way to Pa and Granny's from up there," Wayne said. I believed him.

My interest in Civil War history had begun in Mrs. Whitmire's fifth grade class, and was stirred even more with my seventh grade trip to the Cyclorama in Atlanta. Naturally, I was captivated by the Lincoln Memorial with its giant, bronze statue of Abraham Lincoln sitting comfortably on what resembled a throne. According to the little pamphlet I read, the memorial was built in the style of a Greek Temple, with thirty-six columns measuring forty-four feet in height. My history books and teachers had spoken of Lincoln's strength of character and wisdom during the country's darkest hour, so I reckoned such a tribute was appropriate to this great leader, who was also referred to as the emancipator. Behind President Lincoln's huge statute was etched:

> "IN THIS TEMPLE AS IN THE HEARTS OF THE PEOPLE
> FOR WHOM HE SAVED THE UNION THE MEMORY OF
> ABRAHAM LINCOLN IS ENSHRINED FOREVER."

"...HE SAVED THE UNION." I only read those words as historical fact then, not fully understanding their significance as I do now.

At the Capitol Building I traced my hands up and down the massive columns and reached down to physically touch the steps where presidents and world leaders had walked. Jo and Nant laughed at me, but I didn't care. The places I had read and heard about were all around me. I could see them in person. They weren't just pictures; they were real, and I could touch them.

Although not historical, I was amused at seeing a man in the U. S currency building reading a sheet of newly printed twenty-dollar bills. I guess he was studying the paper money for defects, but he looked so casual, you would have thought he was reading the Washington Post. It seemed like a good job to me. I'd enjoy looking at money all day long.

As we continued our walking tour of the capital, on every street corner was a statue, memorial, or monument honoring a national hero or event dating back to the founding of America. I was wide-eyed and full of wonder. It was like a historical fantasyland.

The staunch, protestant Deaton family did not support the Catholic, John F. Kennedy, in his 1960 presidential campaign, but with the rest of the nation, we were riveted to the events surrounding his assassination in November of 1963. Our feelings toward President Kennedy had softened somewhat, so the next day we made our way to Arlington Cemetery to see his gravesite. It may have been as much fascination as it was paying our respects to a dead president, but still we went.

My idea of an eternal flame was an ostentatious, ten-foot-tall blaze shooting forth from the ground like a gigantic blowtorch.

Instead it was a simple, unassuming flicker softly burning in the center of President Kennedy's resting place. "This is the eternal flame?" I thought. "Looks to me like a puff of wind would blow it out." But it was a peaceful, dignified site. A simple flame intended to burn for the ages in honor of a great American.

I loved that trip to D. C. It made a huge impact on me. I didn't think of it as such then, but later I realized that on those two days in our nation's capital I saw memorials to two presidents who were assassinated one hundred years apart. Both Presidents strove to bring equality and justice to an oppressed people.

I hope we as a country will always work for the rights of all people. I hope we will work to bring people together as equals. I hope we will celebrate our differences and that our differences will unite us rather than divide us.

Those are some of the things that make America great.

Falling water

I'm not sure what prompted our next vacation destination. I think Daddy had heard about Niagara Falls from an army buddy of his during World War II, because Daddy had talked about the falls for years. So the following summer our family piled into Wayne's red and white '57 Chevy and headed north. As is the case with so many natural wonders, pictures only begin to describe the majesty of Mother Nature, and Niagara Falls was no exception.

Our tour guide at the falls told stories of hundreds who had plunged over for one reason or another—some as an act of suicide, and some who were simply crackpot daredevils riding over the falls in wooden barrels. Yes, wooden barrels! Unbelievably, in 1901 the first person to take a barrel ride was a 63-year-old schoolteacher. But for me, the most sensational plunge was not in a wooden barrel or any kind of vessel. It took place in 1960 when, as the result of a boating accident, seven-year-old Roger Woodward—with no protection and wearing only a life jacket and a bathing suit—went over the Canadian Horseshoe Falls, yet lived to tell his story.

As I wrote this part of my memoir, I began to wonder what happened to Roger Woodward. So, as we are prone to do in this era of instant knowledge, I did a Google search. In my brief online research, I learned there are similarities between my story and Roger's. For one, I live in Tennessee and Roger lives in the neighboring state of Alabama, only a couple of hours away. Roger also grew up in a blue collar family and wore hand-me-down clothes. And although I never experienced anything nearly as traumatic as plunging over Niagara Falls, I have faced significant challenges in my life. In a figurative sense, the stream I have swum against for a good portion of my life cannot compare to the literal stream young Roger fought at the base of the falls, but we both defied the odds to try and do something positive with our lives. Roger came close to losing his life that day in 1960; I came close to never finding mine in 1949 when Mama was forced to drink Daddy's homemade miscarriage potion while she was pregnant with me.

Some call Roger the miracle boy. I guess we're both miracle boys.

As we crossed the footbridge through the mist of the falls, our guide pointed out an island with a funny sounding name: Goat Island. She explained that a man used the island to raise a herd of goats during the 1770s and 80s. During the extremely cold winter of 1780, all but one of the goats died. That alone seemed to be a good enough reason to name an island after a hardy goat. Our guide went on to say that as cold as the winter of 1780 was, in March of 1848 it became so cold it caused the gigantic rush of Niagara Falls to freeze solid, and her flow was completely stopped. I couldn't imagine it then, and I can't imagine it today.

Later that night we drove over to the Canadian side of the falls, where they appeared even more spectacular as brilliant colored lights were shined on them. While we were in Canada, I mailed a postcard to my friend Robert Phillips. Below his street address in Walhalla, South Carolina, I wrote "U. S. A."

After all, I was in another country.

The soda jerk

There were two drug stores in Walhalla: People's Pharmacy and Bells Drug Store. Dr. Bell, a respected pharmacist and the original proprietor, opened Bell's Drug Store in 1923. He proudly proclaimed his apothecary, "Bell's for the Best." He successfully ran his business until the late 1930s, when he sold it to Dr. Gilmore. Since "Bell's Drug Store" had such a familiar and inviting ring to it, the name was retained under new ownership but with one exception: because it was no longer owned by Dr. Bell, the possessive apostrophe in the name was omitted. Thus, Bells Drug Store.

A similar reason may be true regarding People's Pharmacy, but I'm not sure. I assumed "People's" referred to an attitude of service rather than ownership—such as a people's pharmacy—serving the pharmacy needs of people.

I know the Bells Drug Store story because I was present when a student approached Sloan Satterfield, now a co-owner of the store, with an offer to renew an advertisement in the high school yearbook, *Walhira*. Sloan agreed to renew the ad, but instructed the student to have the erroneous apostrophe removed from the name of the store because it was no longer owned by Dr. Bell. I don't know whether it was grammatically correct or incorrect, but it's an interesting story—to me anyway.

Each store had its unique qualities, but one was pretty much on a par with the other. However, customers' allegiance to one over the other was much like the allegiance to a brand of automobile. Had the drug stores been cars, People's would have been a Ford, and Bells a Chevrolet. And everybody knows that a true Ford man would rather walk than drive a Chevy, and vice-versa.

People's Pharmacy was satisfactory for filling doctors' chicken-scratch prescriptions, and it carried an excellent inventory of Band-Aids, hot water bottles, liniments, lotions, and everything else one would expect in a modern apothecary. In addition to basic health supplies, fine perfumes and colognes were displayed in lighted glass cases. They even sold Russell Stover Candy.

Bells Drug Store carried a similar line of merchandise, but when it came to the soda fountain, Bells was far superior, at least in popularity.

During the 1950s and '60s, drug store soda fountains were as popular as flat top haircuts. The soda fountain was as important as the prescription pick-up counter, if not more so. Most fountains were like little self-contained diners, placed in the high customer traffic area of the store. Customers gravitated to the bar and booths for a soft drink and a pack of crackers, or sometimes just a cup of coffee. It was a regular gathering place.

On weekdays, the fountain was a popular spot for employees from Main Street businesses to meet for a mid-morning break. Some stood around the marble counter or leaned on display cases, while others sat in the green and white wooden booths. For these fifteen minutes or so, everyone claimed equal status, as dime store sales clerks, office secretaries, attorneys, and bank tellers expressed opinions on politics, world events, and local gossip. At noon, minced barbeque on a toasted bun, served with a bag of potato chips and a cherry Coke, was a lunchtime favorite.

During football season old codgers, some of whom never attended the Friday night game, made themselves at home in booths on Saturday morning. Chugging down cups of coffee for a full hour or more, each armchair professional argued every play, coach's decision, and referee's call, and then guaranteed his game plan would result in a sure win the following week.

But the best soda fountain customers were the 3:30 after-school crowd. City kids from senior high swarmed into Bells and hovered like bees around a beehive. Girls dressed in button- up blouses, pleated skirts, bobby sox and saddle oxfords paired with boys in oxford shirts, Levis and cordovan penny loafers for an afternoon rush of sugar and juvenile hormones. Their young bodies were tightly packed cheek-to-cheek in and around booths with no shame or reticence; some sitting, some standing, others leaning in with not an inch of space for modesty. Between sips and munches, youthful decadence was at its height, as teenagers breathed the intoxicating air of adolescence while suffering the sweet suffocation of amorous desires.

"Are they going steady?"
"When are you gonna ask her out?"
"Was that you 'n Carolyn kissing in the hall?"
"What are you gonna tell your mama?"
"Where's that new drive-in in Seneca?"
"Why was Linda crying in the bathroom?"
"Is Mr. Dupree gettin' married?"
"Where you want me to meet you?"
"Did Gary quit the football team again?"
"What are you wearing to the party Saturday night?"
"How'd you get that bite mark on your neck?"

These were the happy days before there was a *Happy Days.*

Helen Smith attended my church and worked at Bells Drug Store as a sales assistant. In addition to Helen, who pretty much worked the main part of the store, Bells also employed two high school boys as soda jerks. Soda Jerk was the nickname given to a boy whose primary job was to work the fountain. Among other things, he was to make and serve milkshakes, banana splits, Coke floats, and nut sundaes. As a tenth grader in mid-puberty, that was my dream job— to be around all those popular city kids after school, trying to look cool while making them think I was cool—serving up milkshakes to pretty girls while dressed in my starched white jacket. Wow!

Neal Alexander and Mish Barnette had the soda jerk positions filled at Bells, but Mish decided to work with his daddy at the Checkerboard Feed Store. Helen told me about the opening, and then was kind enough to put in a good word for me. Although I had a part-time job working after school at Castles Five and Ten, I wasn't making much money, and my social life had not taken off as fast as I had hoped. I interviewed for the job at Bells on Thursday, and was told to begin work the following Monday. After school and on weekends, I would make seventy-five dollars a month, and during the summer when I could work longer hours, a hundred dollars a month. Compared to the fifty-five cents an hour I was making at Castles Five and Ten, the money seemed more than fair, and the fringe benefits were priceless.

Dr. Gilmore, who owned the controlling interest in the store, was a tall, kind, and gracious Southern gentleman. Every year just before Christmas he took a twenty-dollar bill from the cash register, gave it to me and said, "Merry Christmas." In 1965, that was a nice bonus for a part-time high school employee.

Sloan Satterfield had once worked for Dr. Gilmore, but their personalities were very different. Sloan contracted polio as a boy, and as a result his right arm had limited use. I suppose he was self-conscious about it, and over time he appeared bitter. He rarely smiled, and even though he and I got along OK, I'm sorry he never seemed happy.

As Dr. Gilmore eased into semi-retirement, Ken Johns, a young pharmacy school graduate, was hired to help fill prescriptions and manage the store. Ken was great. He and I had a very cordial working relationship that developed into a genuine friendship. Ken married Juanita Burrell, a cousin of mine on my mother's side. Years later Ken opened his own drug store, Ken's Pharmacy, on Main Street. Ken and I remained friends (and kin) until March, 2016, when after a lengthy illness he passed away at age 74.

And then, there was Dr. Jenkins. He didn't actually work *at* Bells Drug Store; he worked at the Medical Center Pharmacy which was owned by Bells and was located adjacent to a doctors' office complex on South Pine Street.

Dr. Jenkins was a loveable old fellow with a jovial personality. Well into his sixties, his short stature and pot belly made him an endearing caricature. After the Medical Center Pharmacy closed each day at five o'clock, Dr. Jenkins delivered the daily cash receipts to Bells. Then, as sure as clockwork, he'd pick up a single package of Bromo-Seltzer, walk to the soda fountain, pour the contents in a paper cup, add water, let it fizz, and drink it down. Dr. Jenkins' hand had a palsy-like shake, but that was no problem because so did his chin. I can still see his hand and chin pulsating in perfect unison as he lifted the cup of Bromo-Seltzer to his mouth. He never spilled a drop. I respected him too much to laugh, but my goodness, it was a scene worthy of a slapstick comedy routine. I watched it every day, and it never got old. It's a fond memory of Dr. Jenkins, and it brings a smile to my face today when I think about it.

I was more than pleased with my job at Bells, and I threw myself into it. I wanted to run the soda fountain as well as I could and also serve customers in other parts of the store. The work was gratifying, but I soon learned I had a lot to learn.

One afternoon a young woman asked me to direct her to the sanitary napkins. I told her we didn't carry napkins, but she might check with Castles Five and Ten. I knew they had a good selection of paper napkins, paper plates and cups, plastic knives and forks, and other party goods.

She didn't even thank me for the suggestion. Just turned and walked out the door.

I guess she went to People's Pharmacy.

As I became more educated about the store's merchandise, I also became more educated in the ways of the world.

I knew about condoms—not by that name—but until I started working in the drug store, I thought you only purchased condoms in a filling station bathroom. Then someone wrote in our high school underground newspaper, *The Squeal Sheet*, that prophylactics—the proper term used then—were now available in the bathroom of the Dairy Queen in West Union. As a soda jerk, I was around ice cream all day so it was rare that I went to the DQ. Guess I never had to pee when I did go, but I assumed what was printed in *The Squeal Sheet* was true, and a man in need could get rubbers there.

There was one particular couple who frequented Bells on a regular basis. Without going into too much detail, I'll just say you wouldn't expect to see either of them featured in a glamour magazine. Nature had been less than fair with this couple. He was normal ugly, but she was in a category all her own. Mercy! I don't mean to be unkind, but she could have been the star attraction in a traveling freak show. People would have paid money just to look upon her face, and very likely would have suffered lingering nightmares afterward.

Occasionally he came in the drug store by himself, and the routine was the same.

"Yes sir, what can I help you with?"

Under his breath, "Pack o' prophylactics."

"Yes sir. What brand? Trojan? Forex…?"

"Cheapest you got."

I loved that job at Bells.

My daddy cussed yore daddy out

D addy woke up on the wrong side of the bed again. It was a Saturday morning. I thought he and I were only going to the Bank of Walhalla to make good on the check he'd given to Mr. Gillespie, the insurance man, on Tuesday. But Daddy had something else in mind.

A good case of amnesia could have served Daddy well, but like the bad penny that keeps turning up, the spiteful memory of Brother Jim returned again and again. Daddy could not forget, and he sure as heck would not forgive this man for his participation in having him kicked out of the church. And this morning, Daddy was on a mission.

As a way to reconcile his disdain for his Church brother, Daddy sought out people of a kindred spirit who also had a common disgust toward Brother Jim.

Daddy's first cousin, Annie Mae Stubblefield, had once been a member of the Walhalla Number Two Church of God, but had not attended for years. Daddy suspected she had been disfellowshipped, and if so, he was certain Brother Jim had a hand in it. Annie Mae was a logical person to begin the "I hate Brother Jim" discourse. Our first stop was at her home.

Annie Mae met us on her front porch. "Mornin' Harris. What brangs you by?"

Daddy took the sanctimonious approach by inviting Annie Mae to attend church.

"Wanted see if maybe you'd come to church this Sunday."

Annie Mae appeared taken aback. "I ain't never going to that church agin!" she declared.

"Well, why not?" Daddy asked.

"I got kicked out!"

This was too good, so Daddy played along.

"I didn't know that. What happened?"

Her eyes glared with hateful defiance as she stood stiff as an ironing board and pushed the words through her clenched teeth and pressed lips. "Why Harris, I was as good 'o Christian as anybody. I wouldn't even drank a Co-Cola, an' Jim an' th' preacher throwed me outta the church."

I didn't know Co-Cola was a sin. I'd seen my Sunday school teacher drink a six-and-a- half-ounce Coke with a pack of peanuts at Turner's Store. I started to ask Daddy about it, but he put up his hand and shushed me.

"Brother Jim?" Daddy asked with feigned innocence.

"He ain't no brother 'o mine!"

She was set to continue with her tirade, but Daddy had the hate fodder he needed for the moment. "I shore am sorry," Daddy said as we backed away, toward the car.

As we slid into the front seat, Daddy said, "Let's go over to Charles and Jewel's. I heard Charles got fired last week."

Charles Addis was married to Jewel, Daddy's sister. Charles fought on the front lines in World War II, and as a result, he often appeared nervous and high-strung. In today's society, Charles would be given every degree of respect and sympathy for his service and the resulting "Post-Traumatic Stress Disorder (PTSD)" for having faced enemy combat. But a kid sometimes sees humor in the most inappropriate places, especially when raised by a parent who revels in making light of the unfortunate conditions of others.

Wayne, Jo, Nant, and I laughed every time our Aunt Florence mentioned Charles Addis' name, when she added, "He fought on the front lines." The family joke was that his full name was not just Charles Addis, but "Charles Addis He Fought On The Front Lines."

Jewel also had characteristics of nervousness and high-strungedness. Maybe it was an un-diagnosed case of "WWWVWFOTFLS" (Wife of a World War II Veteran Who Fought on the Front Lines Syndrome). Whatever it was, she had a touch of meanness in her.

Charles wasn't home when Daddy and I arrived, but it didn't matter. Jewel pushed the screen door open wide with the news that Charles had gotten fired from his job last Thursday.

Charles was a bricklayer on a building site where Brother Jim was the construction superintendent. I suppose Charles' anxious nature clashed with Jim one time too many, and Jim gave Charles his walking papers. Jewel was, to put it mildly, none too happy about it.

But, as any good mother would, she knew it was important to prepare her daughter for a possible embarrassing situation.

Jim's son, Dexter, rode the school bus with Charles and Jewel's daughter, Wanda. Jewel said, "I told Wanda that if Dexter says 'My daddy fired yore daddy,' you come back with 'Yeah, but my daddy cussed yore daddy out!'"

At school, I had heard my share of cuss fights, and I knew what it meant to get cussed out. I also knew there was no greater defeat than to get cussed out, and no greater victory than to cuss out another person. To fully appreciate the weight of "gettin' cussed out" you either have to have been the cuss-ee or the cuss-er. Once you've been cussed out, there is no recourse. It don't matter what you did, or what's been done to you.

You can shoot a man's best huntin' dog and think you've outdone him. But if he cusses you out, it's over. He's won. Cheat him out of twenty dollars, but if he cusses you out, the account is settled. The cuss-er has been repaid his twenty dollars by the cuss-ee, and with interest.

And yes sir, fire a man from his job. But if the fired man cusses you out before he takes his tools and heads for home, you'd might as well just shut up about it. You're whipped.

"Charles cussed ol' Jim out, did he?" Daddy asked Jewel.

"He shore did. Cussed him out right to his face, and the SOB had to take it, too."

Charles Addis cussed out Brother Jim.

Mission accomplished.

Daddy loved it.

He grinned all the way home.

But there was no one

H e was just weird. Really weird. At least that's what all the students at Walhalla High School thought about Eddie Foster. In the mid-1960s, descriptive words such as nerd, dweeb, geek, and dork were not in the adolescent vernacular, but if they had been, Eddie would have been the sum total of all such descriptors— and to the 10th power. He was the quintessential "weirdo" and no one dared be caught in the most casual verbal exchange with Eddie for fear of also being labeled a "weirdo." I do not remember Eddie ever having even one friend.

For the high school population, Eddie was the modern day social leper whose silent cry was "un-cool, un-cool" with the subtext, "Stay away for fear of attracting my social affliction." Eddie's introverted personality caused him to appear awkward, out of place, inappropriate, and above all, most un-cool. He rarely, if ever, looked anyone in the eye. He wore glasses as thick as Coke bottles. He was pale, short, bent, and carried himself in a semi-recoiled posture. When he spoke, Eddie's voice was low, slow, and muffled, as though speaking to himself, perhaps because no one else would speak to him. He was the kid the bullies loved to pick on, and Eddie had no defense.

As an adult, Eddie perhaps would have been accepted by his peers with no more than a passing thought to his lack of social graces. But Eddie was no adult. He was at that worst of ages, young adolescence; a high school sophomore with a desperate need and desire to be accepted, just as we all were at that age. But no one dared befriend Eddie, because when you're in high school you are judged more harshly than ever by the friends you keep, and Eddie was off-limits.

Eddie's parents were educated, sociable, and respected in Walhalla. His father was a local attorney, and both his father and mother were engaging and somewhat gregarious. But Mother Nature sometimes plays cruel tricks on her innocent children, as it was obvious that Eddie had neither inherited nor learned any positive social traits from his parents.

On occasion, Eddie made feeble attempts to gain attention. Like the time when he brought the disgusting "plastic puke" to school and then pretended to throw up in math class. Had it been anyone else, he would have gotten a big BWAAAAHA! But this was Eddie, and to acknowledge Eddie's practical joke was to also acknowledge Eddie, and Eddie was a "nobody." The nobody that no one dared associate with.

You might expect Eddie to be a bookworm, perhaps lost in his own private world of science fiction—a George McFly type from the movie *Back to the Future*—but Eddie also had a normal side. He was a huge college football fan. Having given up on peer acceptance, Eddie put his hopes in what he believed to be a sympathetic teacher, as he tried to impress Miss Hughes with his knowledge of football trivia. I overheard the chance conversation between Eddie and Miss Hughes after our fifth period English class. Eddie forced a shy smile while relaying the story of the most lopsided score in the history of college football, when in 1916 Georgia Tech routed Cumberland College by a score of 222-0. But Miss Hughes was no sports fan and she, like others, dismissed Eddie with little more than raised eyebrows and a non-committal sigh. Eddie had failed again in his efforts to have someone validate his existence on earth. There was no escape from his hellish prison of isolation and loneliness.

Two bullies from the mill hill, Donnie McPhearson and his brother Richard, took great pleasure in bullying the smaller, weaker boys, and Eddie was their favorite target. Donnie, the older of the two, had flunked two grades and Richard had also flunked a grade, which obviously made them older. They were also bigger, tougher, and meaner than the other boys in our sophomore class. During pickup scrimmage games, Donnie and Richard delighted in roughing up Eddie who, clinging to a thread of self-pride, laughed off the "late hits," and other "no calls." He had no choice but to accept "unnecessary roughness" as part of the game.

There were also the structured P. E. classes, where students performed a series of calisthenics, followed by two laps around the perimeter of the football field. After each race around the field, Coach Wilson, who had no tolerance for weakness, had the three who finished last—the three slowest—run though what he called "The Meat Line." And poor Eddie came dragging in last every time.

By today's standards the meat line would be condemned as politically incorrect, but in the 1960s it was commonly used among southern high schools as a motivational tactic, to force the weak and the slow to try harder. The meat line was a human corridor made by two lines of boys standing a few feet apart, facing each other. As treatment (or punishment), the three slowest victims were to run through the perilous passage as their fellow students slapped them around the butt and thighs. It was pretty much all in good fun for everyone, and even the unlucky threesome laughed it off as a harmless display of testosterone. Everyone, that is, except the McPhearson brothers. To them, it was another chance to dish out punishment.

On one particular day, the unfortunate three finalists reluctantly positioned themselves at the threshold of the corridor. Todd Pearson took a long, deliberate swallow, slowly raised his shoulders, and then made a mad dash through the swatting hands.

Bruce Williams was next. Working the crowd, he snorted and pawed the ground with his foot like a mad bull facing a matador. Then the menacing passageway raised the chant, "Bruce! Bruce! Bruce!" He revved his nerve up a notch, and ran the gamut with nothing bruised except his young male ego.

And then it was Eddie's turn. But Eddie showed no display of feigned histrionics. Although humiliating, he knew his role and played it well. He was Eddie the slowest. Eddie the weakest. Eddie the clumsiest. He was also Eddie the frightened. He had reason to be frightened, because Donnie and Richard McPhearson were waiting at the end of the line to take their cheap shots.

Eddie halted...his eyes grew wide as saucers...his body stiffened like a mannequin...his face contorted into that of some alien creature. As he gazed in stoic silence down that stretched hallway of hell, he looked like a wax figurine from a house of horrors. There was no chant of "Ed-die! Ed-die! Ed-die!" Even in that moment, he was alone.

Finally, with no drama, Eddie made his awkward lunge forward.

Donnie's and Richard's eyes danced with evil delight as Eddie lumbered forth, struggling to dodge the stinging slaps of his classmates. As Eddie approached, Richard faked a high smack, causing Eddie to instinctively raise his hands in defense, while Donnie drove his fist into Eddie's nuts. The punch was so painful there was no laughing it off this time. All self-pride and self-respect vanished as Eddie bent double, grabbing his crotch in excruciating agony.

Among peers, it is the accepted rule that a teenage boy does not cry in front of other teenage boys—ever. But the pain was too much for Eddie. He sobbed like a helpless child. His eyes were wild with fright. His entire persona cried out in unabashed pity, "Won't somebody please help me?" But there was no one.

Years later, a sobering reminder of Eddie came to me during a performance of Handel's *Messiah*, that compelling masterpiece which, for many, is the musical epitome of God's love and redemption for humanity.

As the tenor soloist sang the words to the recitative, "All they that see Him laugh him to scorn," scenes from my high school days began to unfold.

There was Eddie in the halls, in the school cafeteria, on the field in P. E. class. Everywhere. All they that saw him, Eddie the un-cool, laughed him to scorn.

Perhaps it is sacrilegious to compare the sufferings of Jesus to those of Eddie, but when the tenor soloist continued, "He looked for some to have pity on Him, but there was no man, neither found He any to comfort Him," then it became personal.

My thoughts shifted to the day of the infamous meat line. The physical pain for Eddie was overwhelming, but the real tragedy was seen in Eddie's eyes as he looked in hopeless desperation for a friend. Someone, anyone, to have pity on him. But there was no one. No one to have pity on him. No one to comfort him.

No friend. No student. No teacher. No one.

And I was one of the no ones.

Car talk

E ven though pickups were considered a blue collar means of transportation, a man's car was his showcase vehicle, and the decades of the '50s and '60s were the golden age of the automobile.

Forget "A man's home is his castle." For those twenty years or so following World War II, a man's *car* was his castle. It was a time of vivid, two-tone colors with matching fender skirts. Bright, shiny chrome trimmed every curve and corner from bumper to bumper, all the way to the crowning hood ornament. Tires were white-walled and scrubbed as clean as a dinner plate. Artwork-designed hubcaps the size of serving platters covered all four wheels and the full-size spare tire in the boot. No expense was spared on lavish seat covers and floor mats. To complete the ensemble, a glass steering knob with a painted scene from a tropical paradise or a scantily clad, well-proportioned woman, adorned the steering wheel. A man's house could be falling into disrepair, but his car was kept in tip-top running order. His yard might need tending, but his car was always neat and tidy.

Nowadays, all cars look the same to me. I can't tell a Honda from a Toyota, or worse, a Ford from a Chevrolet. But I could identify the make and model of every Ford and Chevy from 1950 through 1969. From year to year, each make of car made subtle changes to tail lights and park lights. A person had to look closely to identify the differences in a 1951 Chevy from those of a 1952, and it took a keen eye to tell the difference between a '55 Ford and a '56.

Automatic transmission was the exception rather than the rule, and each car maker had its own specific name for its brand of automatic transmission. So rare was this extra feature, that car makers displayed the designation in chrome letters in a prominent place on the body of the car. For example, on Chevrolets it was Power Glide, and for Fords, Ford-O-Matic.

Car-themed songs ruled much of the rock 'n' roll charts during the '50s and '60s. Car races, car chases, car crashes, death, and broken hearts were common song themes. It's believed the car-themed song, "Rocket 88," was the first ever actual rock 'n' roll song. One of the more popular songs was "Maybellene," a song by Chuck Berry about a cheatin' woman and a race between a Ford and Cadillac. The Beach Boys recorded quite a few including "409," "Fun, Fun, Fun," and "The Little Old Lady from Pasadena."

"Dead Man's Curve" was a dramatic tear-jerker about a race between a Corvette Sting Ray and a Jaguar XKE. The Jag lost the race and its driver lost his life. As the song says, "You won't come back from Dead Man's Curve."

At age sixteen, I failed to negotiate a sharp curve and totaled my 210 model, blue and white '56 Chevy. Unlike the driver in "Dead Man's Curve," I survived the crash with only a scratched elbow and a broken spirit.

It was on a Saturday night. A group of youth from our church was meeting at seven o'clock for a party at a lodge in Salem, a small town a few miles away. My job at Bells Drug Store kept me at work until 8:00, but at 8:01 I sped from the parking lot and drove with foolish fury. I straightened out the curves by taking the inside lane until I encountered one that was too sharp to straighten. My Chevy skidded to the right, and as I fought to gain control, it fishtailed left, right, and then left again before turning over and starting to roll. This was long before cars had seat belts, so I gripped the steering wheel with all my strength. On the third roll I was shaken loose, so I clasped my hands over my head and buried my chin in my chest. Finally, my Chevy stopped rolling but rested upside-down. The front windshield was completely broken out, so I crawled through with my scratched elbow.

By this time a crowd of onlookers had assembled on the side of the road. Stunned and in a state of semi-shock, I asked if anyone knew my daddy, Harris Deaton. Fortunately, someone did, and he went to fetch him.

"We'll get your car tomorrow," Daddy said when he arrived. "Let's go home."

When I saw Mama, I could tell she had been crying. She asked Daddy how I was. "Solemn as a judge," Daddy said. "Only a scratch." Wayne had heard the news and came home to see about me. The doctors' offices had been closed for hours, but Daddy called Dr. Booker at his home and asked if he'd look me over to make sure there were no internal injuries. He asked Wayne to take me to Dr. Booker's and, if I checked out, drive me out town to take my mind off what had happened. And that's just what Wayne did. He was the same big brother who had always been there for me.

I didn't know what to expect, but Daddy came through that night. He was my daddy. No yelling. No questioning. No condemnation. Just genuine concern for his son.

My blue and white 210 Chevy was a total loss, but all was not lost. I escaped unharmed, and with a bitter-sweet memory of what's important in a time of crisis.

Family.

"...but you will"

While stationed in England during World War II, Daddy was befriended by a group of kindhearted people at the Elim Pentecostal Church near Coventry, pastored by Frederick H. Squire (1904-1962), an international evangelist and pioneer who founded over eighty Pentecostal churches.

Daddy had fond memories of his time overseas. He was aware of what his military service meant to him, and was grateful for the opportunity to see a part of the world he would never have seen. Daddy once said that if it hadn't been for the Army, he'd never have gotten out of Oconee County.

I can't fully appreciate the sacrifice he and so many others made for our country, but books, stories, and movies have helped me realize the cost of freedom. Several years ago I tried to express my gratitude to Daddy for what he and his generation had accomplished. As a free American, I owed him that. His response was the same as so many World War II veterans: "Well...I did my duty. I served my country." I respected him for that.

He was obviously proud of his service, and I'm convinced that for the first time in his life he felt a sense of self-pride. An American soldier stationed on foreign soil was a person to be honored and respected. Daddy must have embraced the recognition, and for an all-too-brief period, gained a sense of self-awareness and self-worth in stark contrast to home, where years earlier he had endured intimidation and abuse. It's ironic that a man finds a safe haven from emotional turmoil three thousand miles away from home during the worst conflict of the twentieth century.

However, after the flag-waving and congratulatory speeches, Daddy was once again forced to face familiar and unfriendly realities. The glimpses of the proud, handsome, young American soldier in uniform were long gone.

Meanwhile, in 1947, Reverend Fred H. Squire founded The International Bible Training Institute (IBTI) in Leamington Spa in central Warwickshire, England. The purpose of IBTI was to train men and women to teach the great truths of the Word of God, and then send them back to their own people. In 1949, Reverend Squire relocated the institute to Burgess Hill in West Sussex. Men and women of all tongues, nationalities, races, and colors came to prepare for fulltime ministry to the uttermost parts of the world.

Reverend Squire died in 1962, but in 1965 Daddy began a correspondence with his widow. He soon placed a trans-Atlantic phone call to Mrs. Squire, who graciously invited him to come for a visit and stay as a guest on the IBTI campus. It's easy to understand why Daddy wanted to revisit the place and people who had welcomed him with such warmth and affection.

As an assembly line worker Daddy never earned a high income, but he was now making a fair wage, and had accumulated three weeks' vacation time. With the help of a loan from Beneficial Finance Company in Anderson, Daddy felt confident he could afford a trip across the Atlantic, and his dream of returning to England might come true. So the decision was made that in July of 1966, he and Mama would take a three-week vacation in the United Kingdom and parts of Europe.

Jo and Nant had both married and moved away. I was in the eleventh grade, and Wayne was a bachelor still living at home. As plans unfolded, the anticipation grew, and Wayne and I decided we wanted to go. Daddy couldn't afford to pay our way, but Wayne was working and had built up a good savings account, so he paid his way, and loaned me money so I could go as well.

In the Atlanta Airport I saw one of the most attractive women I'd ever seen. She was black. Fascinated by her beauty and the fact that she was black, I stared at that beautiful lady until she cut her eyes toward me. It was the most pleasing embarrassment I'd ever experienced.

This was my first time on an airplane, and except for Canada when we went to Niagara Falls, I'd never been outside the country. We flew from Atlanta to John F. Kennedy Airport in New York City, where we spent the night at a nearby hotel. The next morning the hotel shuttle service took us to the Pan-American terminal, and we boarded our flight for London.

The flight took six hours. We flew over three thousand miles, but once we were in the air it felt as if we never moved. We landed at London's Gatwick Airport in the early evening. Everything was foreign to me. If I'd had a dog named Toto with me—as did Dorothy in *The Wizard of Oz*—I would have said, "Toto, we're not in South Carolina anymore."

Five years earlier, Mrs. Earle had told her students we would see for ourselves the places we would study in her sixth grade class. Mrs. Earle's prediction came true much sooner than I ever imagined. There I was on a three-week, eight-country European excursion.

People talked differently, they drove on the wrong side of the road, the weather was much cooler than at home, and they ate differently. Fish and chips was their version of fast food, only their chips were not the kind I was used to. Instead of potato chips, these were more like French fries, and they sure were good. And the money. Forget about dollars and cents. It was pounds, crowns, shillings, and pence. Wayne and I thought it was funny when Daddy, wanting to use a public phone, asked a passing Englishman if he had change for a half crown.

From Gatwick Airport we took the train to Victoria Station, then to Hayward's Heath and on to Burgess Hill, where we hailed a taxi to IBTI. By this time, it was late and we were exhausted, so after a brief welcome Mrs. Squire showed us to our bedrooms. Mama and Daddy shared a bedroom in the main house just off the parlor, while Wayne and I slept in bunk beds in an upstairs room.

Everything about the place reeked of old country charm. Unlike in America, nothing was new. Not even a hint of shiny chrome and slick vinyl could be found among the dark, warm wood, and soft, upholstered furniture. In the parlor we found oversized wing chairs and sofas, ideal for an afternoon nap. Even during the most casual conversations, proper English with crisp diction was enunciated with intention, unlike at home where slang words were common and spoken with a lazy drawl. There was a sense of "proper" manner of behavior which, although quite different from the laid back American style, I found graceful and appealing. Merry old England was already casting her spell on the teenage kid from rural South Carolina. I was falling in love with everything British. And it was only going to get better.

I had heard of the British tradition of afternoon high tea, and on our first morning, I learned of another of their traditions called "elevenses." Every morning at about eleven o'clock, the British take a break for coffee and biscuits—but not the kind of breakfast biscuits I was used to, those served with red-eye gravy or sorghum molasses. What they called biscuits were what we called cookies. We were invited to share "elevenses" with Mrs. Squire and some of the IBTI staff, which included Mrs. Squires' daughter, Dorothy, her husband, Jean Jacques Zbinden, and John and Doreen Wildrianne.

As Wayne and I were preparing to listen to war stories from twenty years ago, there was a polite knock on the parlor door. The students at IBTI had heard of our arrival, and a tall distinguished student dressed in coat and tie pondered, "Would our American friends (Wayne and me) like to join us for coffee and biscuits?" An immediate "Yeah!" shot from Wayne's mouth. He and I were both anxious to meet people closer to our age. I can't say our motives were altogether humane—we had our own notions about European girls—but we were also very curious about English and European cultures.

And this was no ordinary white, southern, American party. As we sipped coffee and nibbled biscuits as sweet as vanilla wafers, we met young men and women from all parts of the United Kingdom, the countries of Europe, and the African continent. Wayne and I bonded with our international friends, and the bond grew stronger during our three weeks' stay.

I fell hard for a pretty, dark-haired French girl, but I didn't know a word of French, and what little English she spoke didn't sound at all like the English I was used to back in South Carolina. We didn't even get to the hand-holding stage. Wayne could have had his pick of girls, but courting was not allowed among students, and surely would have been forbidden between a student and a visiting American. So we kept our distance and suffered in silence.

Roger Miller's hit song "England Swings" was popular in the states and proved to be an accurate description of merry ol' England.

We toured the majestic Westminster Abbey, where for centuries monarchs were crowned to rule the British Realm. In the Abbey I stood on the very spot where George Frederic Handel, composer of the masterwork, *Messiah*, was buried. I was so fascinated with the neo-gothic architecture of Big Ben and the Houses of Parliament that I must have taken a complete roll of film from every possible angle of those grand edifices. At the gates to Buckingham Palace, we viewed the changing of guards whose heads were topped in fur helmets the size of bushel baskets.

In all—including the small country of Luxembourg, through which we only traveled on the train—we toured parts of eight foreign countries: England, France, Scotland, Ireland, Germany, Switzerland, Belgium, and Luxembourg. And castles everywhere. What kind of people lived in these enchanted castles?

As impressive as the famous historical landmarks were, nothing compared to the natural beauty of the spectacular snowcapped Swiss Alps. A real-life picture postcard. And the local color of folks as they bought and exchanged produce and goods at the market on the border town of Aachen, between Germany and Belgium. Wayne and I were amused at peasant women with two-foot-long loaves of bread shoved under their arms like stove wood. With all the wide-eyed wonder of our experiences, the wax-textured toilet paper was only a minor inconvenience.

A not-so-minor inconvenience was our ferry ride across the English Channel to the French coast. Everyone (and I do mean everyone) on board became violently seasick. A local said he had crossed the Channel for thirty years and he had never seen it as bad. The choppy waters were bad enough, but when everyone started throwing up, the nauseous smell was overwhelming. No one, not even the most seasoned seaman, could have taken that pungent odor. Dry land was never so appreciated when we finally docked near Calais, France.

In Paris, I saw the Eiffel Tower with my own eyes and was amazed at how tall it was. We spent the better part of a day at the

Palace of Versailles, where four kings name Louis once reigned. The last of the four, King Louis the Sixteenth (with Marie Antoinette of "Let them eat cake" infamy) was in power when the peasantry revolted resulting in the French Revolution. Louis and Marie were rudely expelled from the palace and were subsequently executed.

It's easy to see why the people revolted. With the royal monarchy surrounding itself in unimaginable splendor and opulence while common French people were starving, the public had no choice but to take matters into their own hands. Louis and Marie were the token nineteenth century French one-percenters who were totally oblivious to the misery of the common folk.

Modern-day American one-percenters take note: I've never been beheaded, but I have a strong notion it is most unpleasant.

Because Daddy had made so many connections during his war years, we had a built-in network of contacts. Friends, and friends of friends, welcomed us into their homes with kindness and doubled as hosts and tour guides. We took an overnight cruise across the Irish Sea and were met by the gracious Christy family from Belfast, who showed us the sights of the Emerald Isle. There I saw where the mountains of Moune sweep down to the sea, and was introduced to the Irish song with the same title. Until then I had never seen a live sheep, but thousands of the white wooly creatures grazed behind stacked stone fences—very different from the barbed wire fences in the states—which stretched through the countryside of beautiful Ireland.

As we flew from Belfast to Glasgow, the stone fences we had seen from eye level were even more charming from our bird's eye view, as they stretched for mile after mile in quadrant patterns across the hills and vales of Gaelic country. Now I understand why the Scots, the Irish, and the Scots-Irish were drawn to the hills of southern Appalachia. In recent years I've had the opportunity to revisit Scotland and Ireland, and each time a longing kindles within me. Call me a naïve tourist, a romantic, or just a fool, but the landscape, myths, lochs, and legends of Scotland and Ireland tug at my heart and soul. I believe I could make a peaceful and contented home there.

I have to give Daddy his due again. I think he knew this was the trip of a lifetime. He wanted us to see as much of the United Kingdom and Europe as our money would allow.

Dr. Gilmore, owner of Bells Drug Store where I worked, had told Daddy our European vacation would be a rich educational experience, equivalent to college level study. Daddy couldn't afford to send me to college. He couldn't afford to pay my expenses for this trip. But through his contacts, dreams, desires, and

Me at 17

determination, he made it possible for me to experience things I would otherwise never have known. That trip across the Atlantic sparked an interest in me to learn about, accept, and be more tolerant of other cultures. Had it not been for that single experience, I might have, as Daddy said about his World War II experience, never gotten out of Oconee County. Sure, I would have physically traveled farther than the county borderlines. I had already done that. But I may never have grown beyond a narrow, provincial mindset, and I would have viewed the rest of the world through very different eyes.

It's been nearly fifty years since Mama, Daddy, Wayne, and I took that trip, but some of the memories are as fresh as this morning's coffee and biscuits.

Winn? What? Why?

T he Winn-Dixie grocery store chain dates back to 1939, when the four Davis brothers bought the Winn & Lovett stores. In 1955, Winn & Lovett purchased the Dixie Home chain and changed its name to the one we recognize today, Winn-Dixie.

Although the name Winn-Dixie had nothing to do with "The War of Northern Aggression," as some called it, anything with the name Dixie in it still warmed the hearts of many old southerners as they clung to the dream of antebellum days and the hope of defeating the hated Yankees once and for all. For them, Winn-Dixie was not only a popular grocery store chain, it was the "business man's special" rallying cry for the rebels in grey.

As a boy, I thought the same. I assumed Winn-Dixie was an alternate spelling of "Win Dixie," a cheer for victory over the Union. Years later I learned the name "Winn" and the word "win" have nothing in common.

Despite its primary location in southern states and a name people associated with a strong allegiance to the Deep South, the Winn-Dixie in Walhalla did something revolutionary: It was the first grocery store to employ black high school students to stock produce and bag groceries. Our local Winn-Dixie may have made an effort toward progress in race relations, but not all the locals were willing to accept blacks in places of business where they directly handled food.

My Granny Dottry told the story of a Mr. Mize, who was checking out at the Winn-Dixie when a young black man began bagging the beans, corn, and potatoes. Mr. Mize lashed out, "Don't you put your black hands on my groceries."

My family's prejudicial attitude was very similar. An African-American man worked all day finishing the concrete on our front porch. He had not eaten since arriving for work that morning, so Mama offered him a bowl of pintos with a piece of cornbread and a glass of ice tea. But those dishes never saw the inside of our house again. After the man finished eating, Daddy told Mama to "throw 'em dishes in the holler." Soap and hot water could not wash away the idea that black hands had touched our white dishes.

Such instances make it obvious that I am personally aware racism is taught by example and learned by experience. For that reason, it is hard for me to condemn good people who, were it not for the influence of bigotry in a society of prejudice, would otherwise have been far more charitable. And not everyone held biased views. There were those who expressed tolerance and a plea for equality for all; good people with the courage to condemn overt discrimination. But bigotry, racism, and intolerance were a part of the culture in which I grew up, and for my story to be complete, it is necessary for me to write about it.

For many of the people I knew, African Americans were believed to be barely a notch above beasts, and some would have treated their beasts better than they treated black citizens. I was repeatedly told that they were unintelligent, evil, cursed (this from the Bible) and dirty.

Some say there are no such things as love and hate, only love and fear. Elisabeth Kübler-Ross takes this notion one step further and says the two emotions are not love *and* fear; they are love *or* fear. If either of these statements is true, then obviously those who did not love African Americans were in fear of them.

Fear?

What were we, the white ninety percent of the population, afraid of?

Were we afraid the other ten percent would rise up and overtake us, and then refuse us basic rights and privileges?

Would we be required, by law, to drink at separate water fountains, use separate bathrooms, and sit in the back of the bus or in designated areas of public places?

Would we be constantly harassed, mocked, and belittled?

Would white boys be hunted, beaten, and lynched over the slightest offense—such as looking at, whistling at, or touching a black girl—all with the blessing of law enforcement?

Were we concerned that an all-black jury would allow egregious crimes by fellow black people to go unpunished and conversely condemn white people to a harsh sentence for a minor offense?

With ten to one odds, the likelihood of that happening was pretty slim. So what were we afraid of?

Obviously, I am writing from a different vantage point now than I would have written in the 1960s, when talk of public school integration was the topic of the day. One of the fears expressed among white parents was that "if they go to school together, they will start to date, and eventually they will get married."

I wish I could say I believed in, and fought for, racial equality, but I am not blameless in my role of bigotry. Although I was not on the frontlines of the bloody fights, the fire hoses, and the attack dogs, I was insensitive and apathetic to the sit-ins, marches, and protests that led to the Civil Rights Bill. Bob Dylan's words to *Blowin' In The Wind* are now a sober reminder of the times I turned my head to pretend I didn't see.

"Don't make fun of 'em; they can't help how they look," was considered a charitable expression when spoken by a white person. As unbelievably racist as that comment was, those and other words or actions of "kindness" toward an African American could get you labeled as a "nigger lover," and that could get you into trouble.

One summer evening our family was sitting on our front porch when a rattletrap truck with two black men stopped in front of our house.

"Can you tell me what time it is?" the driver called from the road.

"Ten after six," Daddy yelled back.

The men immediately drove away, but before they were out of sight, Daddy said, "I was just fixin' to tell you to get the shotgun, Wayne." Such was the paranoia caused by the mere presence of black men.

The Friday night auction in Pickens was a fun way to spend an evening. A huge crowd sat in bleacher-like rows as the auctioneer sold everything from baby doll clothes to used cars. As a roll of Naugahyde crossed the auctioneer's stand he began by saying, "We got twenty yards of nigger hide—I mean Naugahyde—for sale here."

The crowd roared in laugher. "We can sell it all in one piece or by the yard. Now who'll start the biddin'?"

"I'll give you two dollars for four yards o' that nigger hide," a man shouted.

Another roar of laughter.

No one else was interested at the time, so among electric razors, car batteries, and dish towels, the Naugahyde was offered up twice more. Each time the auctioneer repeated, "We got yards of this nigger hide—I mean Naugahyde—for sale."

The crowd laughed louder each time.

Where was I? In the crowd laughing with my family.

All the public schools in the Walhalla district—Salem, Tamassee, Keowee, and Blue Ridge (the black school)—were scheduled to consolidate with the Walhalla schools beginning in the fall of 1965. Before the consolidation, which would obviously result in integration, most discussions regarding the transition took place in private conversations. Lots of mixed and confused feelings were expressed. Some were in favor of integration, but many were opposed. One of Blue Ridge High School's star football players would be attending Walhalla High, and some were looking for any possible excuse to keep him off the varsity team. But decent people were willing to speak up with common-sense opinions. I was working in Bells Drug Store when a potato chip salesman said, "Why, they're crazy! A great player can help the team win. Why would you not let him play?"

Mrs. Collins, my science teacher, asked our class what we thought about Negroes going to school with us. Oddly enough, Dallon Weathers, the same boy who led the chorus, "Oh when the South shall rise again..." on our trip to the Cyclorama a few years earlier, spoke up and said "If that's what it takes for them to get a good education, I think they should be allowed." Other than that, I do not recall a school assembly where the principal, or any official, explained that this is the law and we must abide by it. Nothing was publically said regarding the fact that students from other schools would become our classmates, and we should treat all of them with respect. Maybe it was believed the less said, the less attention would be drawn to the situation.

To the dismay of many, the public schools did consolidate and integrate. On the first day of school the tension was so thick you could cut it with a butcher knife, but not one incident or disruption occurred. There were under-the-breath jokes and murmurings, but except for a nervous atmosphere, everything was a normal first day of school. Unlike some southern communities, no outside agitators arrived to stir up trouble.

Racism is taught and learned, but tolerance can also be taught and learned. During my first semester at Lee College, I was discussing racial issues in a typical bull session with a bunch of guys. From the core of my superior whiteness, I said I could not be friends with a black person. (I don't need to tell you I didn't say "black person.") For the first time in my life, something happened and I remember it to this day. An upperclassman asked a simple yet compelling question: "Why?"

Never before had I been challenged to explain my beliefs. I had been raised in a society where racism and bigotry were not only accepted, they were celebrated.

I didn't have an answer for this upperclassman, so I began to question myself. Later, during a student-led worship service at Lee, my eyes were opened a little wider to an attitude of acceptance and understanding. A ministry student said in disgust that we give money to support our brothers and sisters in Africa, yet we refuse basic rights and privileges to our black brothers and sisters in our local churches, hometowns, and neighborhoods.

We have come a long way. In 1965, no one would have believed this country could ever elect an African-American president.

But the fear, and the questions, remain.

Judy

Disclaimer: My wife, Suzy, said I should write this. It's a part of my past that should be told truthfully.

W here does it all begin?

In elementary school you secretly pass a note to the girl who sits next to you in class. On it is written, "I love you. Do you love me?" Underneath your profession of love are the words "yes" and "no" with a hand-drawn box by each word. If you are lucky, the cute girl will check the box next to the word "yes." I still remember one of my first such experiences. Her name was Doris. She was beautiful. She checked "yes."

The next question is a little harder to pinpoint. When does that elementary school kind of love end and another kind of love begin? It usually happens sometime in the seventh grade, when something bites you with no warning and changes you forever. One day you're having the time of your life playing touch football with the boys. The next day it's the soft touch of a girl's hand that sends you into outer space. It's as awkward as heck. You know you're hooked, but you wouldn't change it for the world.

In junior high I was so shy and insecure I didn't dare make the first move. If only my shy nature had been perceived as playing hard to get, my odds might have been better at attracting a girl. I thought my luck might change on our school field trip to Atlanta. After seeing the Cyclorama exhibit, our class went to nearby Grant Park where there were gags and games for kids. For one of the games you paid a nickel, then gripped the handle of this thing that resembled a huge, floor-mounted thermometer. The stronger your grip, the higher the mercury-like liquid rose to determine your personality.

Billy Darby went ahead of me. He squeezed until the meter rose all the way to the top. "Exciting!" read his personality, and all the girls around agreed with their "wows," "oohs," and "ahs."

I had big hands. I had milked our cow hundreds of times, and I was confident of my strong grip. I was sure I would also score an "Exciting!"

I plopped in my nickel and immediately gripped as hard as I could, but the handle gave no resistance. Maybe I didn't give the machine time to reset from the previous player, or it malfunctioned, or it was all supposed to be a joke. But as I continued to squeeze, the meter only rose to "Sour."

A sour personality. There were no "wows," "oohs," and "ahs." It was more like "Eeeew, sour."

My chance at proving I was exciting vanished in a flash. My self-esteem took a nosedive.

By the time I reached tenth grade, I was recognized for my musical talent, which brought me some attention and helped bolster my confidence. I started asking girls out, and I was lucky enough to have dated some of the most charming ladies in school—at least one who could have been a Miss South Carolina. But I was still so hung up on submitting to our church teachings, I didn't have much to offer a girl in the way of a fun evening.

Take her to a dance? No. Against the church teachings.

Take her to the movies? No. Against the church teachings.

Take her to a ball game? No. Against the church teachings.

After a hamburger, French fries, and a Coke at Linda's Drive-In, all that was left was to cruise Main Street. Well, that is unless you took a ride through the countryside for a nice change of scenery—in more ways than one. There were a few girls (I won't reveal any names) a guy could take to a secluded spot...park...and share...well, tender affection. I will say no more.

But even tender affection was no promise of a second date. There was a popular song which asked, *When will I see you again? Is it my beginning, or is it the end?* When I called for the second date, the question "When will I see you again?" was answered with something like:

"Sorry, I have other plans."

"I'm going steady with Bob now."

(I always loved this one.) "My cousins are coming in from out of town."

Cousins from out of town? God Almighty! Do you think I'm a darn fool?!?

I didn't need to ask "Is it my beginning, or is it the end?" I knew the answer: "The end."

My love life took a turn for the better on September 3, 1966, during my junior year of high school. My first date with Judy. She was a kid I had grown up with, and it seemed I had known her all my life. Our families were friends and had shared an occasional picnic together. Judy and I attended the same church, rode the same school bus, and attended the same high school, so I saw her a lot.

On a date with Judy

I began to notice Judy as more than "just that kid I'd known all my life" at a party at her cousin Shelby's house. As part of a game, we were paired to take a walk together—a sort of cheap imitation of the old-fashioned cake walk. As we walked and talked about school, our favorite songs from the top 40, and who was at the party, Judy said there was someone she always hoped would be at every party. She didn't say it was me, but I got the hint and that was the nudge I needed. Not long after, I asked her for a date.

Playing Putt-Putt was on the fringe of "worldly amusements" but not entirely frowned upon by the church. Walhalla didn't have a Putt-Putt course, so I drove Judy and me to the closest one in Anderson to take in a game. Neither of us was any good, but playing well was not a priority. As we chased the golf ball along the greens with our putters, Judy said something about us and next week. I jokingly accused her of asking *me* for a date; a girl asking a guy for a date was something unheard of in the mid-'60s. We laughed about the role reversal, and it was then that this lovely sophomore with a beguiling smile, dancing eyes, and dimples as big as quarters began to capture my heart.

The following spring, I wrote in Judy's yearbook that she was "the reason I keep my shirt tail in, my clothes neat, and my hair combed…You're the reason for the smile on my face, and if it's not on my face, it's in my heart." My goodness, I was mushy. Yep. I had it bad.

As we grew closer, we shared everything. Of course we shared precious moments; we were teenagers in love. We also shared our deepest thoughts about life, living, emotions, hopes, and dreams. Eventually there was a bond between us so strong I thought it would never be broken. We exchanged pictures. She wore my blue jacket. I asked her to go steady with me. She wore my high school ring. We had the usual tiffs all young lovers have, but we knew they were just chapters in the book of love.

At school, Judy and I stretched our morning break between second and third period as long as possible before returning to class. We ate lunch together, and between classes we squeezed in a passing caress. I was always late to class and was repeatedly sent to the principal's office, but I didn't care. Teenagers in love know what's important, and everything else is inconsequential. On the school bus, we sat as close as two people can sit. We talked about our friends, school, classes, teachers, but more than anything, we talked about our feelings. In the evenings we spent hours on the phone, and after hanging up we tuned to WOWO radio station in Fort Wayne, Indiana. We imagined our hearts and souls meeting and soaring across all time and space to the honey-toned, lush sounds of The Association, as they sang, "Cherish is the word..."

Judy's grandmother, Granny Loudermilk, was a widow in her nineties, and someone needed to spend nights with her. Judy loved her Granny and was glad to offer her Granny-sitting services, but Judy's motives were not entirely altruistic. Granny Loudermilk lived down the road, over a hill, and out of sight from Judy's parents' house. We knew they wouldn't spot my car on week nights as I turned into Granny Loudermilk's driveway, so we planned frequent mid-week rendezvous.

We dated throughout my junior and senior years of high school, as well as the year I was living at home while attending Central Wesleyan College. During those three years we began to imagine a future together.

After three years we were insanely in love, but we did have enough gumption to know we weren't ready for marriage. As our intense feelings competed with sound reason, we began to feel overwhelmed. Neither of us wanted to say it, but we needed some time apart, and the fall of 1968 presented a common-sense solution. I was making plans to attend Lee College in Cleveland, Tennessee, a four-hour drive from home. To relieve some of the tension, and to give ourselves some breathing room, Judy and I made the difficult decision to see other people while I was at Lee, as she finished her senior year of high school.

Our agreement was that we would date others while I was away, and anytime I came home on a weekend we would plan to see each other. It was a scary, painful decision, but we assumed it was right. We convinced ourselves that if our love was steadfast it would stand up to this test, but we also questioned, would absence really make our hearts grow fonder?

Before leaving for college I was so confused. I expressed my mixed emotions of hope, doubt, dread, and concern as I wrote in Judy's yearbook, "I think everything will be f

ine when I return… I hate myself for going away but I guess we'll be better in the long run, won't we??…I think it will do us both a lot of good and make us grow up some…I'm going to miss you terribly, terribly!"

With four hours' distance and no car, I was away for weeks at a time. Although the male- to-female ratio at Lee College was in favor of the females in numbers, it was much in favor of the males when it came to dating possibilities. I wasn't that much to look at, but my singing helped attract the attention of some beautiful young coeds and, on occasion, I hit paydirt. With Judy's looks and personality, and now with me out of the way, guys lined up in droves for a chance with her.

On those rare occasions when I came home, we tried to pretend things were the same, but it was obvious our relationship was changing. It was different. The ease and gracefulness we once felt now seemed a bit awkward. The deep, abiding love we once shared was less convincing.

In the fall of 1969 Judy enrolled as a freshman at Lee, but due to a lack of funds I remained at home to work. Now she was the one going away to college. We knew our relationship was not the same, but we were still holding on as we tried to convince ourselves we could recapture that spark we once had. While at home, I began dating a very attractive young woman I met at work, and Judy became infatuated with a psychology major at Lee. The bond that was once so durable was unraveling, even as we desperately clung to the past and tried to pretend otherwise. Eventually, we accepted that it was hopeless to continue.

We made a couple of attempts to reconcile and thought again that we might have a future together. At one point, we even started planning toward marriage, but by then too much had happened; too much time, space, and other people in our lives. Something was missing and we couldn't make it work. We'd lost that lovin' feelin'. It was gone, gone, gone.

Judy and I married—but not each other—and moved on with our lives. Once when I was at a very low point and desperate for someone to talk to, I confided in her. After all we'd shared in the past, I knew she was the person who understood me better than anyone else. My world was shattered, and Judy was there for me. She listened as I poured out my broken heart to her. She was an angel that day. I can never express how fortunate I was, or how grateful I was to have her as my best friend.

Judy earned a master's degree in counseling but fell in love with teaching. After completing her education, she moved back to Walhalla to pursue a career as a special needs teacher, now retired after twenty-seven years. On occasion, Suzy and I see Judy in passing when we are home for a visit. We enjoy catching up on family, children, and grandchildren. Sometimes we even talk and laugh about the "good old days."

I admire and respect Judy. She and I are friends. We always will be.

My vehicle

M y love of singing began when I was seven years old. I sang "He's Got the Whole World in His Hands" on a Sunday night at the Cherry Hill Church of God. I still remember how good I felt when I was complimented by Dawson Alexander, an older buddy and "branch kin".

Once Daddy made reconciliation with the Walhalla Number Two Church of God, our entire family became members there, and so began many years of singing in my home church, other churches, and countless other venues.

I learned early that singing was one thing I could do, and I loved it. Singing brought me so much attention that on some level, even at a young age, I knew singing would be my ticket: the vehicle that would carry me through life.

Music was a big part of every service in my church. At a typical service the choir would sing four, five, maybe six songs. The presiding preacher would then announce, "The choir might come down. Now we'll have our special music." Depending on who was available, special music was a mini-concert of solos, duets, trios, quartets, maybe even a quintet.

We went to church four times a week, which allowed me ample opportunities to sing. My Aunt Gertrude (Gert), a fine musician, was the church pianist. I remember with great fondness practicing and performing with Gert for our regular church services, revivals, and every church-related event in and around Walhalla.

My talented aunt, Gert

Some people say church made a significant impact on their personal life. I agree that church impacted my personal life, and it also impacted my professional life. Church provided me a platform where I gained invaluable experience that would not only prove beneficial during my youth, but also continued throughout my career as a professional singer.

As a kid, "He's Got the Whole World in His Hands" was a cute song and a big hit for me, but as a teenager, my repertoire expanded to classic gospel hymns, such as "Wonderful Peace," with its comforting words:

> *Peace, peace, wonderful peace,*
> *Coming down from the Father above;*
> *Sweep over my spirit forever I pray,*
> *In fathomless billows of love.*

The poetic phrases and majestic melody in "How Great Thou Art" was, and remains, an enduring favorite. Converts also related to the beloved song, "Ship Ahoy," as it portrayed a poor drowning soul rescued by the good Captain, Jesus:

> *I was drifting away on life's pitiless sea,*
> *And the angry waves threatened my ruin to be,*
> *When away at my side, there I dimly descried*
> *A stately old vessel, and loudly I cried:*
> *"Ship ahoy! Ship ahoy!"*
> *And loudly I cried: "Ship ahoy!"*

But the song that stands out most from my early years of singing is titled, "It's Real." The verse speaks of a Christian in doubt that his sins are forgiven, but the refrain reassures him that all doubts are settled, and his salvation is secure.

I was the star soloist in my high school chorus. Miss Brandt convinced me I was the best thing since a new 64-pack of Crayolas. With a disparaging parent, and a church that fostered self-deprecation, my self-respect was a constant struggle. Due to my stern upbringing, I resented not being allowed to experience many of the fun activities in which other students participated. However, those limited experiences "forced" me to focus on music. It was the one thing I could do. I had nothing else with which to identify other than singing. Miss Brandt, with her glowing compliments and persistent praise of my talent, made up for my self-doubt and self-conscious personality. It didn't hurt that during "senior superlatives" voting I was unanimously chosen by my class as "Most Talented."

My major in college was never a question. There was nothing but music for me. And music was enough.

During my senior year of high school, a representative from our county Vocational Rehabilitation office made a visit to Walhalla High which proved to be a defining moment in my life. The representative explained that any student with a disability could apply for financial assistance to attend college.

I had badly injured my knee in a Sunday afternoon backyard football game and had sought relief from every doctor in town, as well as an orthopedic specialist in Anderson. When I told my friend, Charlie, that maybe I could get money to attend college, he said if anyone in our class would qualify, it would be Jo Ann Rogers, a classmate who had polio from childhood. Nevertheless, I knew this was the only way I would be able to attend Lee College, a Church of God institution in Cleveland, Tennessee. My one and only choice of schools.

Remember when I was in the sixth grade and heard the Lee College Touring Choir in concert at the Walhalla Number One Church of God? They performed great anthems, standard classical choral works, and beautiful hymn arrangements. Their concert was a program of high quality music that was moving and powerfully worshipful. Although it seemed like a dream, I knew then that Lee College was where I wanted to attend, and I knew I wanted to study music there.

Over the next six years, when singing in other churches and talking to friends at youth camp and camp meeting, I began to realize that the narrow church teachings I had been taught were not so rigidly enforced in every individual church. For some, it was as though they didn't exist. Boys at larger, less rural churches played on their public schools' sports teams. Girls in similar churches were involved in various school activities. Some were even cheerleaders.

But what was Lee College like?

Larry, a friend from church, had just graduated from Lee with a degree in music education. Larry often told me how much he loved it there, and that the culture was very different from the environment in which we had grown up. He assured me that the music program was superb and I would receive excellent training.

Despite my resentment toward what I perceived as ridiculous teachings, my basic beliefs in the doctrine of the church had not changed. I was more convinced than ever; if at all possible, Lee was the place for me.

I had nothing to lose by applying for financial assistance, so I completed the paperwork and turned it in to the Vocational Rehabilitation office. Incredibly, they not only helped with my college tuition and fees, but also paid for surgery to repair the torn cartilage in my right knee.

Surgery on my knee was scheduled for mid-August, so I deferred my application to Lee and attended a college closer to home. For two semesters I took courses at Central Wesleyan College (now Southern Wesleyan University) in Central, South Carolina. Central Wesleyan was a fine school, and fortunately it was only about twenty miles from home, an easy commute. As a commuter I did not have the expense of room and board, but at home there were too many distractions and negative influences. By my second semester I was making plans to attend Lee, and although my grades were borderline, I was accepted. With Vocational Rehabilitation's financial assistance, I entered Lee in the fall of 1968.

Before I arrived as a student, I had never once set foot on the Lee College campus. The previous summer, I worked in construction and saved some money to buy a few clothes, towels, and toiletries to make the transition to Lee. I guess I should have worked more and saved more, because on that first day at Lee I had eight dollars in my pocket. Even in 1968, eight dollars wouldn't buy much.

In the week before I moved, there was no celebration dinner, no farewell or good luck party given by my family or by anyone. Even Judy and I didn't do anything special to mark this next chapter in my life. We shared every possible minute together clinging to each other while, at the same time, trying to let go.

On the day I left home, neither parent drove me to Cleveland. No one was present to help me move into my dorm room. No one bid a tearful goodbye and waved from the car until it was out of sight.

I didn't own a car then, so I hitched a ride with Larry, who had left some of his belongings in his dorm room at Lee and needed to clean it out before the new students began arriving on Monday. We left for Cleveland on Sunday afternoon, August 11, 1968.

Truth is sometimes stranger than fiction. It was in the yard of Brother Jim, the man whom Daddy disliked so much, that I was playing football and injured my knee. That injury resulted in financial assistance from Vocational Rehabilitation, which made it possible for me to attend college. And Larry, my friend who gave me the ride to Lee College, was the son of none other than Brother Jim. Irony can sure be amusing and render poetic justice.

Lee proved to be everything I had hoped for. It was well removed from the judgmental, oppressive environment where I had lived for nineteen years. And although it was a conservative Christian school, Lee provided a much-needed social life that I had never known. Young Christians whom I grew to admire and respect were aware and interested in current events beyond the narrow confines of the church. Classmates, faculty, and staff looked, dressed, acted, and spoke as well-rounded,

My freshman year at Lee

intelligent people. Most women cut and styled their hair, wore makeup and jewelry, and were fashionably dressed. Lee had a winning intercollegiate basketball team—with real cheerleaders. Guys sat up until the wee hours playing cards while talking about sports and girls.

Lee was a different world. A place I had so desperately wanted and needed. The social void in me was finally being filled. As I played catch-up on social life, I neglected course work, and for the first couple of semesters, I barely scraped by. But there was always music, my voice, my singing.

Had I not had talent, I doubt I would ever have completed a baccalaureate degree, and certainly not a graduate degree. Due to academic and financial constraints, it was necessary for me to take a temporary hiatus from college from time to time. It was pretty much study a semester, then go home and work a semester. I took several detours, and nearly lost my way a few times, but I never stopped dreaming. I always knew that someday, somehow, I would eventually receive my diploma.

Jim Burns was my voice teacher at Lee. In a different way, he was my Miss Brandt. Mr. Burns, as I called him then, gave me sound instruction, challenged me to be better—much better—and constantly reassured me of my abilities. His passion for classical music and his vision of greatness for me broadened my horizons.

About midway through my first semester of study, Mr. Burns, seemingly from out of the blue, asked me, "Have you ever considered singing opera?" In my mind I thought, opera?! As a South Carolina country boy, I had never seen an opera, but my preconceived notions were stereotypical.

To answer his question, "No." Singing opera had never occurred to me, but now I was intrigued. I had been recognized as a fine singer, but opera? This would put me in an elite category.

A well-known quote states, "When the student is ready, the teacher will appear." I was ready, and my teacher appeared.

Mr. Burns became Dr. Burns and later just "Jim" as he and I developed a close personal bond and eventually served as colleagues on the music faculty of Lee University. I will always be grateful to Jim for his direction, influence, and friendship.

My final word...for now

As described in my "Up to the Forks of the Road" chapter, a very rich part of my childhood was lived on that half-mile stretch from the end of our driveway up to the forks of the road. As I think back over the years, I am aware of how the forks of the road metaphor continued its prevalence throughout my life. Many times I made a conscious decision to go in a different direction than was expected. As the traveler in Robert Frost's poem, *The Road Not Taken*, I often took the road less traveled, and that has made the difference. I was determined to pursue specific goals in my life; to follow my passions regardless of what others thought or said. When the popular choice was to take the right fork in the road, I took the left one because that's where my hunger led me.

Home, no more home to me
Whither must I wander?
Hunger my driver
I go where I must.
      Robert Louis Stevenson

My choice of vocation was often misunderstood, but I was undeterred. I knew in my heart why I was put on this planet. Music was a hobby until I became a young adult; then it evolved into an intense passion. My decision to follow the path of vocal performance was an unpopular one. For instance:

In my mid-thirties, at the encouragement of a trusted professional, I made the decision to audition for major roles in Austrian and German opera houses. Had I been offered a contract, it would have been a dream come true. When I told an aunt of my decision to audition, her response was, "What you wanna do *that* for?" Another relative actually said, "I'm gonna pray real hard that you don't get that."

I won't dignify that ludicrous comment by saying my relative's prayer was answered, but despite spending five weeks auditioning in Europe, I was not offered a contract. However, with a lot of hard work, determination, grit, and taking the less-traveled road, I did sing opera—a lot of opera—throughout a large part of the United States.

Once when I was having an especially good stretch of performances, I was required to travel for several continuous weeks. While I was away, Daddy called our home and asked to speak to me. Suzy explained that I was out of town on a singing engagement and wouldn't be back for several more days. His response was, "How does he hold down a job, being gone so much?" Suzy tried to explain that singing *was* my job.

He never got it.

On another occasion, I was on tour with an opera company and a performance took me near my home town of Walhalla, so Mama and Daddy came to see me. (Note I didn't say they came to *hear* me.) After the show Mama, Daddy, Suzy, and I went to Hardees for hamburgers. Once we were seated in a booth, Daddy was careful to tell me the ticket lady at the theatre let Suzy in to see the opera for free, but he and Mama had to pay.

As Falke in *Die Fledermaus* with Knoxville Opera Company

How do you respond to such a statement?

Not once during our meal did Mama or Daddy say they enjoyed my singing, the music, or any part of the opera production. They did, however, tell me how much money Wayne was making as a cookware salesman and that he'd recently bought a new Cadillac.

I've always been proud of Wayne, and I was glad he was doing so well. I also knew Mama and Daddy didn't understand or appreciate opera. I didn't expect much, but I was their son, too, and I was sitting right in front of them.

That's the price you pay when you travel an unfamiliar path.

After approximately twenty years as a professional singer performing major operatic roles, working with renowned artists, singing as a soloist with symphony orchestras, and presenting literally hundreds of concerts in countless different venues throughout the country, Daddy told me that I should cut a record because I could sing "as good as Conway Twitty."

I didn't believe him. I never cut a record.

Me with some of my classmates, when I performed at the Walhalla Civic Auditorium. L-R: Robert Phillips, Jane Rogers, Charlie Morgan, Ann Wilson, me, Brenda Stephens, Annie Bailes, Stephen Blackwell and Bill McLees (high school names)

I am now sixty-seven years old. I can hardly type those words, much less believe them. Age sixty-seven seemed beyond the age of death when I was the boy I write about in this memoir. But here I am, healthy in body, mind, and spirit.

In December of 2015, my darling Suzy and I celebrated our thirty-seventh anniversary. Ours is a very good marriage. Not perfect, but whose is? We both have strong personalities that clash on occasion. But not for long. Our love causes us to forgive and enjoy the life we have left together.

With Suzy

Because of Suzy I have a stepson, Greg, whom I could not love more or be prouder of if he were my own flesh and blood. Greg is smart and a very hard worker. He is a partner in a successful architecture firm in Knoxville and is married to Jen, a beautiful, intelligent woman whom Suzy and I adore.

It gets better. I have two grandsons, Spencer and Andy—my best buddies. They will never know the impact they have made on me. Before Andy was born, Mama said, "Spencer is the best thing that ever happened to you." And in many ways, he was. Then, four years later, another "best thing happened" when Andy came along. Their personalities could not be more different, yet I love them the same.

I have a long way to go, but I am a better person because of Spencer and Andy. I have learned a lot from teachers, role models, and mentors, but Spencer and Andy have taught me what is really important in life.

My beliefs regarding certain aspects of what some call "religion" have changed considerably over the years. I was raised in a racist, prejudiced environment. Self-righteous judgment was a common theme expressed in everyday conversations and proclaimed from church pulpits. I grew up to the tune of "Give Me That Old Time Religion" with the words, *Makes me love everybody*. But in truth, it was *Makes me love everybody who is like me—White, Protestant, and Pentecostal*.

I have come to the conclusion that to question is to learn. To learn is to grow. To grow is to change. And I welcome change as a part of my growth.

In a rare serious conversation with a brother-in-law, I was reminded that love of God and love of neighbor are the two essential truths in virtually all faiths. As a Christian, I find that philosophy confirmed in these words of Jesus: *You shall love the Lord your God with all your heart, with all your soul, and with all your mind. This is the first and great commandment. And the second is like it: You shall love your neighbor as yourself. On these two commandments hang all the Law and the Prophets.*

Matthew 22:38-40

So, who is my neighbor? You are. No matter who you are. You are.

Mama used to say, "It takes a lifetime to learn how to live." In about thirty years I'll have it figured out. Look me up then, and I'll tell you all about it.

Wayne, Jo, Nant and me in 2016

Made in the USA
Columbia, SC
22 April 2017